Pennsylvania's

4th Edition

RAILS - to - TRAILS
CONSERVANCY

Rails-to-Trails Conservancy,
Pennsylvania Field Office

Published by Rails-to-Trails Conservancy
1100 17th Street NW
Washington, DC 20036
202-331-9696

ISBN 0-925794-14-7

Printing by Jednota Press
Middletown, PA

Maps and Book Design:
Steve Spindler Cartography
Steve Spindler and John Boyle
Philadelphia, PA
www.bikemap.com

Cover Design: Peter Volz

Acknowledgments

The 4th edition is a continuation of fact gathering by many people over the last several years. Those individuals include but are not limited to Lori Kieffer Yeich, Pam and Bill Metzger, Julie Larison, Craig Warner, and George Ely. Finally, our heartfelt thanks to the many rail-trail organizations, municipalities, and state and federal agencies who also provided us with information and who design, build and maintain the many rail-trails we enjoy.

Introduction

Imagine a network of trails across Pennsylvania connecting our cities, towns and countrysides. Locally, this network would link our neighborhoods with our schools, workplaces, shopping areas and parks, helping to serve community transportation needs as well as meet the growing demand for close-to-home recreation.

To help you experience this wonderful resource, *Pennsylvania's Rail-Trails* contains information on more than 700 miles of rail-trails, including maps, photographs, directions, and historical background. In this edition, we are proud to offer our readers the opportunity to take advantage of trailside amenities. This is only a beginning. We entered into this new domain by contacting those businesses who are friends of the Pennsylvania Field Office. In future editions, we plan to include others as requested. On some of the maps you will see icons depicting bed and breakfasts, restaurants, campgrounds and bike shops. On these maps, you will find the name and phone number of the business. In the back of the book you will find an index of the trailside businesses listing additional information. Finally, we have also listed the websites and e-mail addresses of some of the rail-trails to further assist you.

With 10,000 miles of rail-trails completed, the rails-to-trails movement is the fastest growing sector of trail development in the country—and Pennsylvania is one of the leading rail-trail states. As such, this book is very much a "living document," which will be updated as new information reaches our office and additional resources become available.

While rail-trail development has been remarkable, thousands of miles of railroad rights-of-way across the nation are being lost to highways, parking lots and haphazard development. This loss takes away a part of our heritage and adds to our sense of isolation from locales very nearby. Throughout our daily activities, we should have the option to walk or bicycle in a safe and pleasurable environment.

I hope this publication will be a small step toward providing you more freedom to choose your mode of travel and to enjoy Pennsylvania's beautiful landscapes.

Tom Sexton, Director
Rails-to-Trails Conservancy
Pennsylvania Field Office

For Your Personal Rail-Trail Notes...

How to Use this Guide

The map on pages 2 and 3 shows the general location of 79 rail-trails in Pennsylvania. The rail-trails are listed in alphabetical order.

Individual trail maps and details about each rail-trail can be found beginning on Page 4. Along with a history of the rail-trail and its highlights, we have included specific information about endpoints, mileage, surfaces and permitted uses.

Services, such as food, lodging and bicycle shops have been noted for some of the trails, both on their maps and in an alphabetical listing on page 136.

Beneath each trail map, beside the page number, is a map of Pennsylvania that depicts where the trail is located in Pennsylvania.

In addition, we have provided the name of a local contact or agency for you to contact for more information about each rail–trail. Some of the local contacts have detailed maps and brochures. On some of the trails, we have also listed the local contact's e-mail and or website addresses. If the trail is shown as under development, the local contact will be able to give you more information about when the trail will be completed.

Please be mindful of your own safety. Wear a bike helmet, and make sure your family and friends to the same.

Activities and Services in this Guide

🚶	walking, hiking and jogging	🎣	fishing access
🎿	cross–country skiing	🛷	snowmobiling
🐎	horseback riding	♿	wheelchair access
🚲	bicycling	🅿	parking available
🚵	mountain bikes recommended	🚲	bicycle shop/rental
🛼	in-line skating and roller skating permitted	⛺	campground
🍴	restaurant/food	🛏	bed and breakfast

Key to Trails

━━━━━━ rail-trail
▬ ▬ ▬ under development
------ connecting trail

Pennsylvania's Rail-Trails

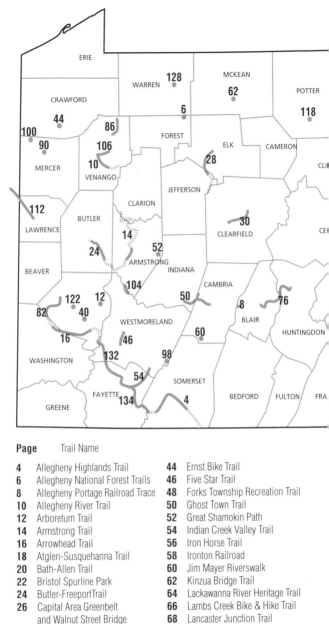

ERIE

WARREN **128**

MCKEAN
62

POTTER
118

CRAWFORD

44

100
90

86

6

FOREST

ELK
28

CAMERON

CLI

MERCER

106
10

VENANGO

JEFFERSON

CLARION

112

LAWRENCE

BUTLER

14

52

30

CLEARFIELD

CE

24

ARMSTRONG

INDIANA

BEAVER

104

CAMBRIA

122 **12**

82 **40**

50

8

76

16

WESTMORELAND

BLAIR

HUNTINGDON

132

46

60

98

WASHINGTON

54

SOMERSET

GREENE

FAYETTE **134**

4

BEDFORD

FULTON

FRA

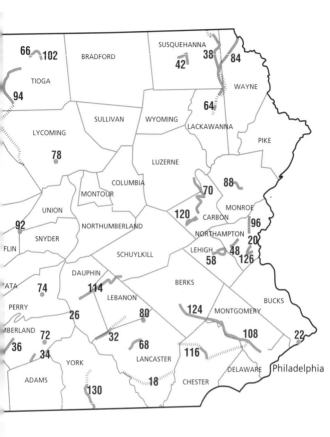

Allegheny Highlands Trail

The Western Maryland Railroad Connellsville Extension, opened in 1912, was a latecomer to the railroad scene. It was part of the "Alphabet Route," an important through-freight route between Chicago and New York, but was abandoned in 1975.

Destined to be a major component of the trail from Pittsburgh to Washington, DC, the Allegheny Highlands follows the Casselman River at an easy grade through the rugged Allegheny Plateau, allowing bicyclists and hikers to travel through the numerous ridges, not over them.

The trail features many reminders of the railroad's past, most notably the half-mile-long Salisbury Viaduct shown here. Just south of the trail is Mt. Davis, the highest point in Pennsylvania at 3,213 feet, and Fort Hill, an ancient Algonquin encampment excavated by archae-ologists in 1939. Whitewater rafting, downhill and cross-country skiing, and fishing can all be found nearby.

From PA Turnpike Exit 10 (Somerset), take US 219 South about 15 miles to Garrett. Turn right on SR653 .2 mile to Berlin Street. Turn left and go .1 mile to right turn just after a bridge. Trailhead parking is .3 miles ahead. For the Rockwood trailhead, follow signs to SR281 south. Follow 281 about 10 miles to SR653 east to Rockwood, where it becomes Bridge Street. When SR653 turns left, stay on Bridge Street over the river. The parking lot is on the right just after the bridge.

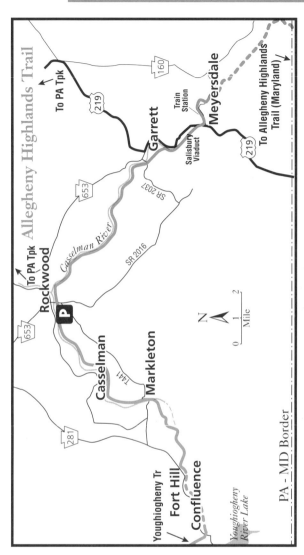

Location: Somerset County
Miles: 16.2
Endpoints: Garrett to Markleton
Surface: Crushed limestone
Contact: Hank Parke
           Somerset County Rails-to-Trails Assoc.
           PO Box 413
           Somerset, PA 15501
           814-445-6431
           www.atatrail.org

Allegheny National Forest Trails

Encompassing half a million acres, the Allegheny National Forest is criss-crossed with numerous hiking trails that take advantage of the many old logging roads, abandoned railroad grades, and utility rights-of-way within the forest. Portions of these trails use abandoned railroad grades. They are listed together for that reason. Most of them follow the Tionesta Valley Railroad, a logging railroad abandoned since 1939.

1   *Allegheny Snowmobile Loop (100+ miles)*
Large loop crossing entire Allegheny National Forest that connects to many communities and Allegany State Park in New York. Marked with orange diamonds.

2   *Brush Hollow Cross Country Ski Trail (6.9 miles)*
Blazed with blue diamonds, skiers with a wide range of expertise will find a challenging experience.

3   *Heart's Content Cross-Country Ski Trail (6.4 miles)*
Loops around stands of ancient beech, hemlock, and white pine. Blazed with blue diamonds.

4   *Kelletville to Nebraska Trace (12.2 miles)*
This trail follows along the long abandoned Sheffield and Tionesta Railroad Grade, which was constructed in the 1880's for lumbering, freight and occasional passenger use.

5   *Little Drummer Historical Pathway (3.1 miles)*
Located in the Owl's Nest area of the Allegheny National Forest, the Little Drummer Histrical Pathway is a designated Watchable Wildlife Area.

6   *Marienville ATV/Bike Trail (36.8 miles)*
Divided into Bike Trail and ATV Trail. Terrain differs between trails. Blazed with yellow diamonds.

7   *Mill Creek Trail (5.6 miles)*
Traverses flat to gently rolling terrain. Connects Brush Hollow Trails with Twin Lakes Trail. Blazed with white diamonds.

8   *Minister Creek Trail (6.6 miles)*
Very scenic trail with interesting house-sized rocks. Has several campsites along Minister Creek and meets with the North Country Scenic Trail. Blazed in white diamonds.

9   *North Country National Scenic Trail (86.4 miles)*
Part of a 3,200-mile National Scenic Trail. Travels along waterfalls, historic areas, and old hardwood stands. Blazed with blue diamonds.

10   *Rocky Gap ATV/Bike Trail (20.8 miles)*
Constructed for ATV and motorbikes. Blazed with yellow diamonds.

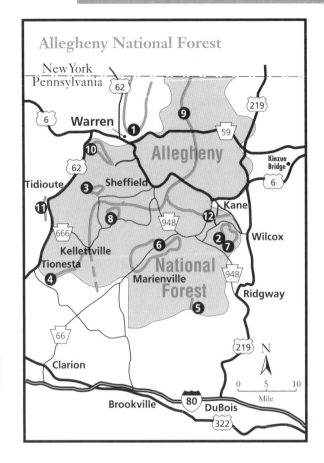

11 ***Tidioute Riverside RecTrek Trail (4.5 miles)***
   The Tidioute Riverside RecTrek Trail runs along the scenic Allegheny River, and boasts a waterfall, valley of ferns and a variety of wildflowers, birds and animals.

12 ***Twin Lakes Trail (15.8 miles)***
   Connects the North Country Scenic Trail with Twin Lakes Recreation Area. Marked with white diamonds.

Contact: USDA Forest Service,
            Allegheny National Forest
            222 Liberty St.
            Warren, PA
            814-723-5150
            TTY: 814-726-2710
            www.penn.com/~anf

Allegheny Portage Railroad Trace

In 1825, the citizens of Philadelphia were agitated. New York's Erie Canal had just opened, draining away much income from the Quaker City. Pennsylvania needed its own canal system—and fast—but the Allegheny Mountains stood in the way.

The Portage Railroad was built as the easiest means then available to connect the east and west sections of the Pennsylvania Canal. Passengers, freight and eventually whole canal boats were pulled by ropes on railroad cars over the Alleghenies on a series of ten steam-powered inclined planes. The system, though cumbersome, survived until 1854.

Although the Portage Railroad has been abandoned for almost a century and a half, many of its structures still stand. The Lemon House—built in 1834 by Samuel Lemon, who became one of the richest men in Cambria County by selling coal, lumber and food to the railroaders and passengers—is located near the summit and open to the public.

The unique Skew Arch bridge, built to carry a road over the Portage, is a marvel of well-preserved intricate stonework. Staple Bend Tunnel, the oldest railroad tunnel in the United States, survives on the western slope of the mountain near Johnstown and is slated for restoration.

To reach the Allegheny Porage Railroad Trace, take the Gallitzin Exit from new Route 22 to the park's visitor center.

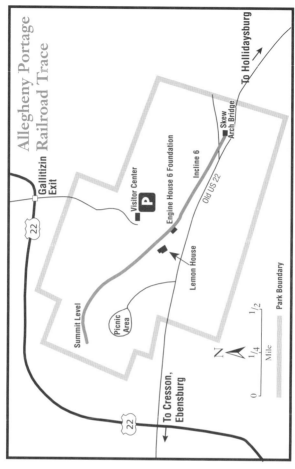

Location:	Blair and Cambria Counties
Miles:	1.5
Endpoints:	Allegheny Portage National Railroad Historic Site
Surface:	Original ballast, grass
Contact:	Joanne Hanley
	Allegheny Portage Railroad National Historic Site
	PO Box 189
	Cresson, PA 16630
	814-886-6150

Allegheny River Trail

The Allegheny River Trail is an extension of the Samuel Justus Recreational Trail south from Franklin, continuing on the abandoned Allegheny Valley line, and following the Allegheny River on a section included in the National Wild and Scenic Rivers system.

After its abandonment in 1984, the line was acquired by the Scrubgrass Generating Company and donated to the non-profit Allegheny Valley Trails Association. This group is building an extensive rail-trails system in northwestern Pennsylvania and hopes to make this trail a part of a bigger network from the Great Lakes to the nation's capital.

Just off the trail is an oil well that once belonged to John Wilkes Booth. About five miles downriver from Franklin is the Belmar railroad bridge (built in 1907), which will offer a spectacular view of the river and valley when the Clarion Secondary trail is completed.

Nine miles further, Indian God Rock, a set of Native American rock carvings, can be found along the trail. The carvings date from 1200-1750 and are listed in the National Register of Historic Places.

In Franklin, take PA8 north to its juncture with US322. Take US322 as it becomes 8th Street and crosses the Allegheny River. Trailhead parking is on the right after the bridge. The parking lot is marked for the Samuel Justus Trail, the northern section of the trail out of Franklin.

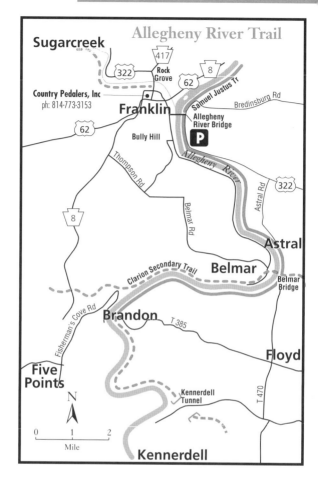

Allegheny River Trail

Sugarcreek

417

322

Rock Grove

8

62

Country Pedalers, Inc
ph: 814-773-3153

Samuel Justus Tr

Bredinsburg Rd

Franklin

62

Allegheny River Bridge

P

Bully Hill

Allegheny River

Astral Rd

322

Thompson Rd

8

Belmar Rd

Astral

Clarion Secondary Trail

Belmar

Belmar Bridge

Fisherman's Cove Rd

Brandon

T 385

Floyd

T 470

Five Points

N

Kennerdell Tunnel

0   1   2
Mile

Kennerdell

  on certain sections

Location:	Venango County
Miles:	10
Endpoints:	Franklin to Brandon
Surface:	Asphalt (first 5 miles)
	Tar & chip (second 5 miles)
Contact:	David Howes
	Allegheny Valley Trails Association
	153 Sixth Avenue
	Clarion, PA 16214
	814-226-6455

Arboretum Trail

From 1853 to 1856, the Allegheny Valley Railroad was built from Pittsburgh to Kittanning, passing right through the heart of Oakmont Borough. In 1903, Oakmont's rail service improved greatly when the Pennsylvania Railroad opened its Brilliant Cutoff, linking the AVR with other sections of the City.

Declining rail traffic in the 1960s led Conrail to close one of the two tracks in the Borough and during the 1970s the inactive track was removed. In 1995, the corridor was sold—back to the Allegheny Valley Railroad!

A shining example of what dedicated volunteers can accomplish, the Arboretum Trail is also one of Pennsylvania's four rails-with-trails, where trains and trail users share the corridor. Conceived by the Garden Club of Oakmont in 1989 as a centennial gift to the community, the Arboretum Trail is a part of Oakmont's Boulevard Project, an ambitious plan for the renovation of a downtown business corridor.

The Garden Club raised $3 million for trail construction, landscaping and renovation to the corridor's surroundings, and long-term maintenance of the plantings installed along the Boulevard. An oasis of green and growing beauty and a tangible asset to its community, the Arboretum Trail is a delight in all seasons.

From the Pennsylvania turnpike, take Exit 5 (Allegheny Valley) and bear right past the toll booth. Follow the signs to Oakmont and cross the Hulton Bridge approximately one mile from the exit. Turn right just before or just after the railroad crossing on Hulton Road, onto either Allegheny Avenue or Allegheny River Boulevard, to find a parking space. The trail lies between the two streets. From downtown Pittsburgh, take Route 28 north to the Blawnox Exit. Continue straight along old Route 28 until you come to the Hulton Bridge on the right. Remember, this is a walking trail only.

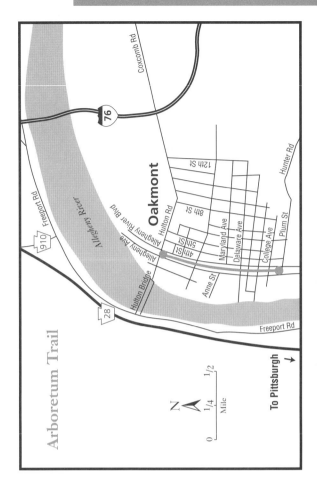

Location:	Allegheny County
Miles:	1
Endpoints:	Oakmont Borough
Surface:	Asphalt
Contact:	Kitty Vagley
	Oakmont Garden Club
	769 Fifth Street
	Oakmont, PA 15139
	412-826-9295

Armstrong Trail

Begun in 1853, the Allegheny Valley Railroad reached Brady's Bend in 1867. Originally built to haul coal, it also became an important oil route after petroleum was discovered farther north. The line was abandoned in 1991. Fortunately, the Armstrong County Conservancy began spearheading an effort to preserve the right-of-way a year earlier and provided funds to start the Allegheny Valley Land Trust. The Trust then secured a quarter million dollar loan to purchase the line from Conrail.

Beginning at Schenley (the former site of the Schenley Distillery), the Armstrong Trail passes by many Industrial Age remnants, such as coke ovens and iron furnaces, the remains of a large resort hotel at Watersonville, and the abandoned Monarch Mines. The trail also features the Brady's Bend tunnel, built in 1915 to bypass a loop in the river, thus shortening the line by about 5 miles.

Parking is available at several places along this 52.5 mile corridor. The easiest to reach are in Ford City and East Brady. The common point is a complex intersection of PA66, PA28 and US422 just south of Kittanning. From the intersection, go left onto SR2011 for about 3 miles to PA128. Follow 128 until it crosses the Allegheny River, at which point you should go straight onto Ross Avenue between the tracks and the river. A Fish Commission boat launch 1 mile ahead just after Rosston provides access to the trail just before Crooked Creek.

For East Brady, go north on South Water Street and cross the Allegheny at Market Street. Turn left at the end of the bridge onto Pine Hill Road until it meets PA268. Stay on 268 north about 16 miles to Kepple Creek and turn right on PA68. Follow 68 about 8 miles, back across the Allegheny to East Brady, where it becomes Third Street. In East Brady, turn right on Grant Street to a left turn on Sixth Street.

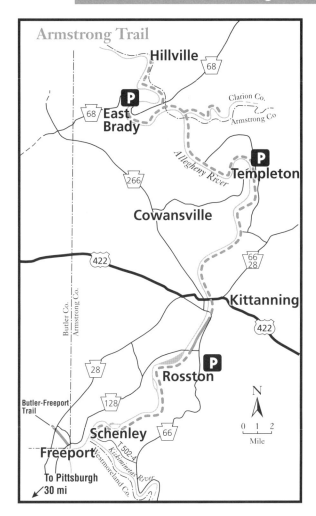

Armstrong Trail

Location:	Armstrong and Clarion Counties
Miles:	52.5
Endpoints:	Schenley to Upper Hillville
Surface:	Unimproved surface, 2.4 miles asphalt/ 1.0 mile crushed limestone
Contact:	Allegheny Valley Land Trust
	Kittanning Visitors Center
	Market and Water Sts.
	PO Box 777
	Kittanning, PA 16201
	724-543-4478
	www.trfn.clpgh.org/avlt/

Arrowhead Trail

Originally, the Montour Railroad carried coal to local coke ovens and provided connections to the Ohio River. It was purchased in 1975 by the Pittsburgh & Lake Erie Railroad (P&LE) and abandoned in 1980. Peters Township then purchased the right-of-way and 100 acres to create the Arrowhead Trail, which opened in 1985.

The Arrowhead Trail received the Excellence in Highway Design Award in a statewide competition conducted by the Pennsylvania Department of Transportation. It's not hard to figure out why the trail won the honor. At the main entrance is a hillside covered with wildflowers, the creation of Giant Oaks Garden Club, which also won three awards. In addition to the beautiful flowers, the township planted 500 trees along the trail.

On a trip along the Arrowhead Trail, you'll travel by wooded and suburban areas and pass through Peterswood Park. The asphalt surface is great for bicycling or in-line skating, and is accessible for individuals with disabilities.

For both the east and west trailheads, travel south on US19 from Pittsburgh to SR1010 (Valley Brook Road) one mile past the Allegheny Washington County lines. For the west trailhead on Pelipetz Road, stay on Valley Brook .5 mile and turn right on Pelipetz. Parking is immediately ahead on the left. For the east trailhead, stay on Valley Brook Road 1.5 miles to SR1002 (McMurray Road) and turn left. Turn right on Brookwood Road (1.4 miles ahead) and then a left onto Brush Run Road, a little under a mile later. This parking lot is on the right just after Scott Road.

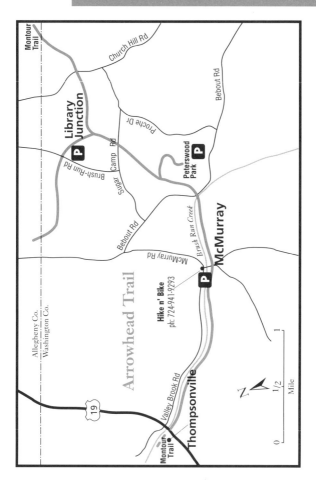

 on certain sections

Location: Washington County
Miles: 3.5
Endpoints: Thompsonville to Library Junction
Surface: Mostly asphalt, original ballast
Contact: Peters Township Parks & Recreation
610 East McMurray Road
McMurray, PA 15317
724-942-5000

Atglen-Susquehanna Trail

The Pennsylvania Railroad's Atglen-Susquehanna Line (also known as the Low Grade Line) was an engineering marvel. Despite the hilly terrain of southern Lancaster County, the line boasted no grade steeper than 1% and no curve greater than two degrees. Built as a freight line to bypass the Main Line passenger service to Philadelphia, construction commenced in 1902 with an estimated cost of $19.5 million. Historic stone bridges, brick-lined tunnels and the 600-foot long, 130-foot high Martic Forge Trestle are a few of the structures whose construction required the talents of laborers of many cultures and nationalities.

We hope the vision of turning this 23-mile railroad line into a rail-trail survives the buffeting winds of local politics. The Friends of the Atglen-Susquehanna Trail refuse to give up their dream. Preservation of the corridor whose construction claimed the lives of 200 workers is believed by FAST and many supporting organizations and individuals in Lancaster County to be a vital part of the County's Open Space Plan.

And what a trail it will make!

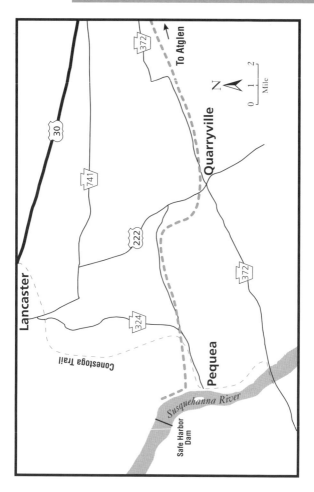

Location: Lancaster County
Miles: 23
Endpoints: Atglen to the Susquehanna River to
        Safe Harbor
Surface: Undeveloped
Contact: Julie Nettke
        Friends of the Atglen-Susquehanna Trail, Inc.
        PO Box 146
        Quarryville, PA 17560
        717-786-9055

Bath-Allen Trail

For 77 years, the tiny Northampton & Bath Railroad traveled the seven miles between the two towns which gave its name. Located in the heart of Northampton County's cement district, the N&B's trains supplied its larger cousins, the Central of New Jersey, Lehigh & New England, and Delaware, Lackawanna & Western, with cement, bringing in limestone, gypsum and coal to US Steel and its successors. Perhaps its most famous contribution to railroad history is its place as the first US railroad to become completely dieselized.

Like its larger cousins, the N&B fell victim to the changing face of transportation and the rise of the trucking industry. Abandoned in 1979, the corridor's purchase by Northampton County's Park Board allows the "little train that could" to continue to serve its namesake towns by connecting their parks (Bicentennial and Jacksonville, as well as a proposed regional park), schools (George Wolf and Jacksonville) and historic centers (Franklin Fort and the Craig settlement, the county's earliest Scotch-Irish community). Plans to expand the trail into both Northampton and Bath are on the county's drawing board.

To reach the trail at Jacksonville Park, take Route 512 south from Bath and turn right in two miles onto Jacksonville Road. The park is just ahead on the right and the trailhead is a few hundred feet ahead on the left.

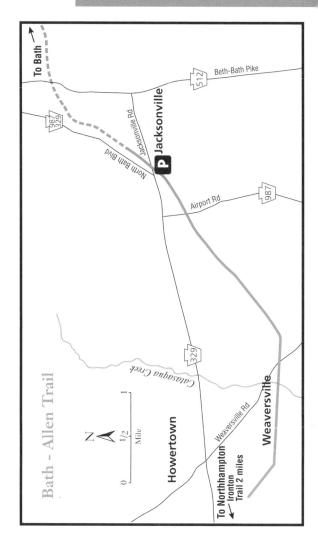

Location:	Northampton County
Miles:	5.2
Endpoints:	Weaversville to Jacksonville
Surface:	Dirt, crushed stone
Contact:	Northampton County
	Parks & Recreation
	RD 4, Greystone Building
	Nazareth, PA 18064-9278
	610-746-1975

Bristol Spurline Park

In 1834, the Philadelphia and Trenton railroad came to Bristol, a bustling little port where the Delaware Division of the Pennsylvania canal system met the tidewater of the Delaware River.

The canal still exists in Bristol, but the original main line of the Philadelphia and Trenton was relocated in 1882 and it became an industrial spur. The relocated line is now Amtrak's New York to Washington main line, one of the most heavily traveled passenger railroads in the country.

Conrail donated the line to the town of Bristol and the trail was opened in 1980.

Traversing downtown Bristol, this residential trail will eventually connect with the canal at Bath Road and with the Delaware River near Green Lane Road. This asphalt-surfaced trail also connects with nearby playing fields, parks, the town's elementary school and retirement communities.

Take PA Turnpike to Bristol exit. Take Green Lane into Borough of Bristol. Then follow Radcliffe Street to Mill Street. The trailhead is ahead on the right; the trail runs parallel to the street.

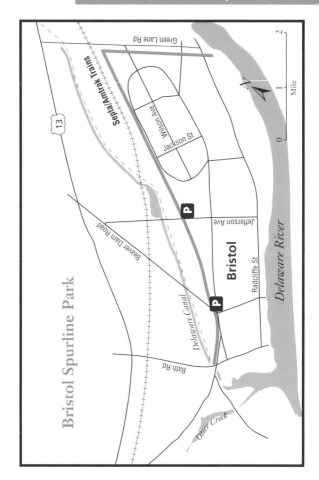

Location: Bucks County
Miles: 2.5
Endpoints: Mill Street to Radcliffe Street, Bristol
Surface: Asphalt
Contact: Borough of Bristol
250 Pond Street
Bristol, PA 19007
215-788-3828

Butler-Freeport Community Trail

In 1871, the first railroad in Butler County started operations. After a two-day celebration for the railroad's opening, a mock funeral was held for the stagecoach that ran between Butler and Freeport.

Built as a branch of the Western Pennsylvania Railroad, the Butler line tapped the high quality limestone deposits vital Pittsburgh's growing steel industry.

Butler soon had a steel business of its own thanks to the new railroad and the line became a conduit for iron ore. It became part of the Pennsylvania Railroad in 1903 and was abandoned in 1987. The trail opened in 1989.

The southern half of the Butler-Freeport Community Trail is nestled in a scenic wooded valley which follows Little Buffalo Creek to Buffalo Creek. Buffalo Creek then flows into the Allegheny River at Freeport. Remains of two stone quarries and some brick kilns can be seen in this southern section.

Heading north from Cabot, the results of late 19th century development are still visible. The former Saxon City Hotel, built in 1871, remains, as does an old, still active, lumberyard.

In using the trail, you should be aware that a disagreement between nearby landowners and the trail group is, as of August, 1998, being litigated. In addition, some sections of the trail may be obstructed or posted. Of course, trail users should always refrain from trespassing or otherwise disturbing a trail's neighbors and this is especially true in the case of this trail. Because the litigation may be resolved at any time, you may wish to check with the trail group about its current status.

From Pittsburgh, take Route 28 north to a left on Route 356 north. Go about four miles to Sarver Road. Bear right and go 1 mile to Buffalo Township. Fire Station on left. Park in upper lot. This access area is three miles from the southern end and seven miles from the northern end of the trail.

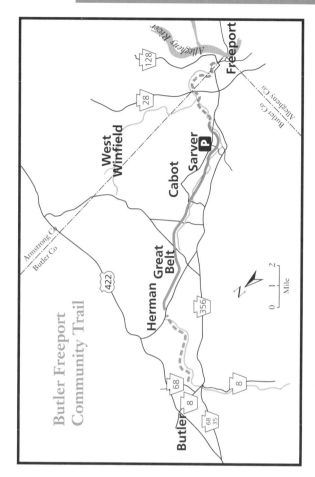

Location:	Butler County
Miles:	12
Endpoints:	Butler to Freeport
Surface:	Crushed limestone
Contact:	Ronald J. Bennett
	Butler-Freeport Community
	Trail Council, Inc.
	PO Box 533
	Saxonburg, PA 16056
	724-352-4783

Capital Area Greenbelt and Walnut Street Bridge

Harrisburg, Pennsylvania's Capital Area Greenbelt is a 20-mile ring of parks and trails encircling the City. Originally conceived by landscape architect Warren Manning (a disciple of Frederick Law Olmsted), the Greenbelt was partially constructed in accordance with Manning's plan through the early part of the 1900s. Unfortunately, the project was never fully realized and much of the Greenbelt fell into disuse and disrepair. In 1991, a group of dedicated volunteers took up the banner for park and trail development and formed the Capital Area Greenbelt Association.

An integral part of the Capital Area Greenbelt is the Walnut Street Bridge, which provides a critical pedestrian link to City Island. City Island is a popular multi-use recreational area in the heart of Harrisburg.

Built in 1889, the Walnut Street Bridge was used as a street car system that survived until 1950, when it was converted to automobile use. In 1972, flood Agnes damaged the bridge beyond repair, and it was converted into a pedestrian bridge. In 1996, icy flood waters removed the western span of the bridge, which will be rebuilt by the year 2000.

A small section of the Greenbelt lies on an abandoned rail corridor, its trains once serving the industries that lined Harrisburg's Susquehanna Riverfront. To reach this portion of the circular trail, travel South Cameron Street to True Temper's Jackson Manufacturing plant. The rail-trail runs along South Cameron.

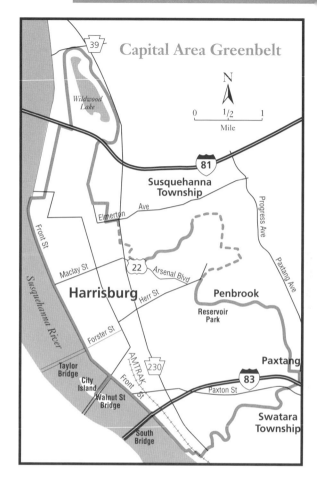

Location: Dauphin County
Miles: 20 (about 2 miles on railroad corridor)
Endpoints: Loop trail around Harrisburg
Surface: Varied: wood chips, asphalt, stone and grass
Contact: Norman Lacasse
       Capital Area Greenbelt Association
       2415 Patton Road
       Harrisburg, PA 17112
       717-652-4079

Clarion-Little Toby Creek

The Clairon-Little Toby Creek rail trail is an 18 mile section of an abandoned rail line built by the Clearfield to Ridgway Rail Company. Built in 1886, the rail line was created to transport lumber and coal from mills to market, but it also included a busy passenger service between Ridgway and Falls Creek. Abandoned in the 1960's, the corridor remained fairly intact under the ownership of Penn Central Corporation. Since 1992, the Tricounty Rails to Trails Association have been busy developing the abandoned line into one of the state's most beautiful rail trails.

The trail meanders along the wild and scenic Clarion River and Little Toby Creek through Elk and Jefferson Counties, between the charming small towns of Ridgway and Brockway. Historical markers along the banks of the Little Toby Creek greet the trail user. These markers commemorate a former stone quarry in which a World War I munitions plant once stood, a Depression-era Civilian Conservation Corps camp which employed 250 men during the lean years of the 1930's, and a number of long-gone ghost towns from the lumbering era. Another fine feature of the trail is a swinging bridge across Little Toby Creek.

Ten miles of the trail are surfaced with crushed limestone, and the remainder is well graded with a cinder base.

To reach the Brockway trailhead from I-80, take SR 219 North into Brockway. Turn left at SR 28. Turn right on 7th Avenue. The Trailhead is at the end of the street, past the community pool. To reach the Ridgway trailhead from I-80, take SR 219 North to Ridgway. Turn left on Water Street, just before Love's Canoe and Market Basket. Continue one block to the trailhead, which is behind the Ridgway Record on Center Street.

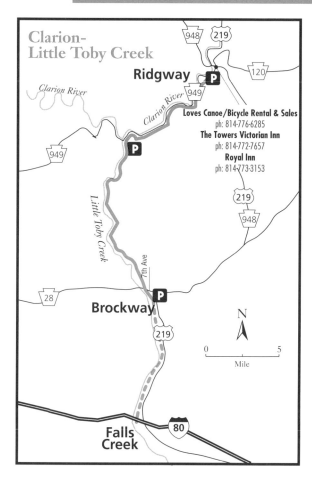

Clarion-
Little Toby Creek

Clarion River

Ridgway

Clarion River

Loves Canoe/Bicycle Rental & Sales
ph: 814-776-6285
The Towers Victorian Inn
ph: 814-772-7657
Royal Inn
ph: 814-773-3153

Little Toby Creek

7th Ave

Brockway

N

0   5
Mile

**Falls
Creek**

Location:	Elk and Jefferson Counties
Miles:	18
Endpoints:	Ridgway to Brockway
Surface:	Crushed limestone & graded cinder
Contact:	Ridgway Chamber of Commerce
	231 Main St.
	Ridgway, PA 15853
	814-776-1424

Clearfield to Grampian Trail

By the mid-1860s, the residents of isolated Clearfield County knew that the health of their economy was inexorably tied to the railroad. If the area's abundant coal was to reach faraway metropolitan markets, their dependence upon wagons and shallow rivers had to shift. The Tyrone & Clearfield Railroad reached the county's border in 1863, but it wasn't until the Pennsylvania Railroad acquired the TCR in 1866 that a connection seemed possible. An association of 75 volunteers was formed to try to extend the railroad to the county seat. In three years the association raised $77,000 and in January 1869 the first train arrived in Clearfield. By Christmas Day 1874, similar efforts in Curwensville brought train service west. It took 18 more years for the railroad to reach Grampian.

Today, this hard won corridor is the Clearfield to Grampian Trail. From Clearfield to Curwensville, the trail follows the West Branch of the Susquehanna River near Curwensville Lake Recreation Area, with modern camping facilities, a beach and water sports. Its limestone surface is suitable for road bikes and wheelchairs. After leaving Curwensville traveling southwest to Grampian, the trail's surface is unfinished and suitable for walking, skiing and mountain bikes. Here the terrain becomes more densely forested and passes near Kratzer Run, a small and pleasant creek. Efforts by Clearfield County Rails-to-Trails Association to develop a finished trail surface in this section are continuing.

To reach the Clearfield trailhead, take I-80 to Exit 19 (Clearfield). Take PA879 south two or three miles and turn right on Spruce Street exit. Take the first left (Chester Street) and in another 200 yards turn left just before the True Value Hardware store. Trailhead is just ahead on the left. Parking is available at the Riverside supermarket nearby during the week; park at the trailhead on weekends.

30

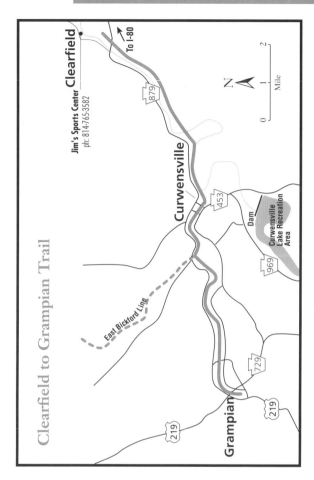

Location: Clearfield County
Miles: 10
Endpoints: Clearfield to Grampian
Surface: Crushed limestone
Contact: Fredric J. Ammerman
Clearfield County Rails-to-Trails
310 East Cherry Street
Clearfield, PA 16830
814-765-1701

Conewago Trail

Built in 1883 by Robert H. Coleman, who was one of the richest men in America at the time, the Cornwall & Lebanon Railroad operated for almost 100 years. This privately owned railroad served the Coleman family well by transporting iron from the family's iron furnaces to the Pennsylvania Railroad, which would then haul the iron ore to the mill at Steelton.

By 1910, there were eight daily passenger trains to the resort town of Mt. Gretna, home of the Pennsylvania Chautauqua and the National Guard encampment. The tracks were abandoned after the Hurricane Agnes flood of 1972, and converted to a trail in 1981.

Shaded by a canopy of trees, the Conewago Trail is a wonderful way to spend your day, whether you like to horseback ride, walk, jog, or bicycle.

Starting out, you will pass the quiet and meandering Conewago Creek, fields of corn, and open meadows. Not long into your journey, you will hear rushing water as you approach a wide creek and large boulders. This is an idea spot to take a break and listen to the water and watch the swirling rapids.

Continuing, you will pass through some pockets of wooded land where you may see deer or grouse. You will also pass a few horse, dairy, and chicken farms. Diverse and peaceful, this trail is the perfect escape.

The most conveniently located trailhead is along Route 230, two miles west of Elizabethtown.

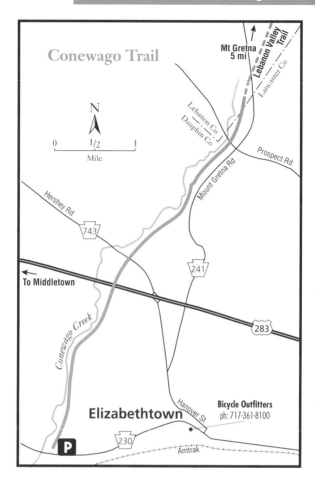

Conewago Trail

Mt Gretna
5 mi

Lebanon Valley Trail

Lancaster Co

N

0   1/2   1
Mile

Lebanon Co
Dauphin Co

Prospect Rd

Mount Gretna Rd

Hershey Rd

743

241

To Middletown

283

Conewago Creek

Bicycle Outfitters
ph: 717-361-8100

Elizabethtown

Hanover St

P

230

Amtrak

Location:	Lancaster County
Miles:	5
Endpoints:	Conewago to Cornwall
Surface:	Cinder
Contact:	Lancaster County Parks & Recreation
	1050 Rockford Road
	Lancaster, PA 17602
	717-299-8215

Cumberland County Hiker/Biker Trail

South Mountain in Pennsylvania actually marks the northern end of the mighty Blue Ridge chain, which stretches south to Georgia. Pine Grove Furnace first began operating in 1764 to take advantage of the relatively small but rich South Mountain iron ore deposits.

Exactly 100 years after the furnace began, the South Mountain Railroad was built to serve it. After ironmaking ceased, the railroad eked out a living hauling slate, sand and tourists. Starting in 1940, the line was abandoned in pieces.

The state forestry department purchased the furnace property in 1911, and it ultimately became Michaux State Forest and Pine Grove Furnace State Park.

About 30,000 people a year use the Cumberland County Hiker/Biker Trail. The trail begins near Fuller Lake which was originally an iron ore pit, and passes relics of the ironmaking era, including the ironmaster's house, the furnace remains, and the original company store, stable, grist mill and inn, now the park office.

Pine Grove marks the halfway point of the Appalachian Trail, which crosses the valley at each end of the Cumberland County Trail. The quarter-mile-long Swamp nature trail and the steep Pole Steeple Trail with its spectacular view of the entire 696-acre park create a trail network with a variety of hiking possibilities.

From I-81, take Exit 11 and proceed south on Route 233 to the state park. Park for the trail at the Iron Furnace's stack pavilion and proceed east to the trailhead.

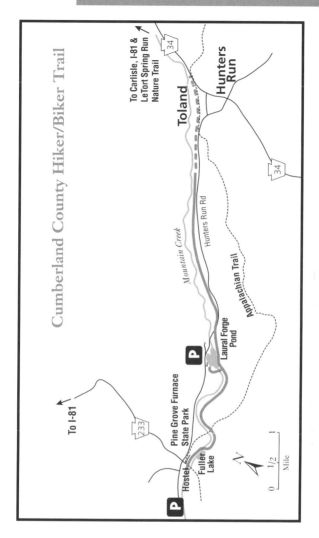

Cumberland County Hiker/Biker Trail

To Carlisle, I-81 &
LeTort Spring Run
Nature Trail

Toland

Hunters Run

34

Mountain Creek

Hunters Run Rd

Appalachian Trail

Laural Forge
Pond

Pine Grove Furnace
State Park

To I-81

233

Hostel

Fuller
Lake

N

0   1/2   1
Mile

Location:	Cumberland County
Miles:	5.5
Endpoints:	Pine Grove Furnace State Park to Mountain Creek Campground
Surface:	Crushed limestone
Contact:	Pine Grove Furnace State Park
	1100 Pine Grove Road
	Gardners, PA 17324
	717-486-7174
	www.dcnr.state.pa.us

Cumberland Valley Trail

Headquartered in Lemoyne, the Cumberland Valley Railroad was first incorporated in 1831. By 1889, its trains carried passengers and freight as far as Hagerstown, Maryland and Winchester, Virginia. The railroad was ahead of its time, running the first sleeping car in the nation and instituting one of the first prohibitions against drug and alcohol use by its employees.

The same sense of pride and close-knit community spirit that led CVRR foremen to offer cash prizes to any child who found so much as a stone out of place along the rail line now guides the Cumberland Valley Rails-to-Trails Council as it works to establish its trail along 11 miles of the CVRR corridor. Not even demolition of four historic concrete arch bridges can temper the group's determination to reconnect the towns of Shippensburg and Newville.

The trail is presently undeveloped and suitable for walking, mountain biking and equestrian use only. Because of the steep embankments caused by the loss of the bridges, some road crossings require extra caution on the part of trail users.

The best access to the trail is at Oakville. From US 11 or PA533, turn west on Oakville Road into the village. Turn left at Beidler Drive and park adjacent to grassy picnic area. The trail crosses Oakville Road along the west side of the picnic area. In Newville, take PA533 south/east onto Cherry Street to McFarland Street. Park along the south/east side of McFarland. Hikers may park at the Shippensburg municipal lot on West Burd Street; however, there is no equestrian or bicycle access in Shippensburg at this time.

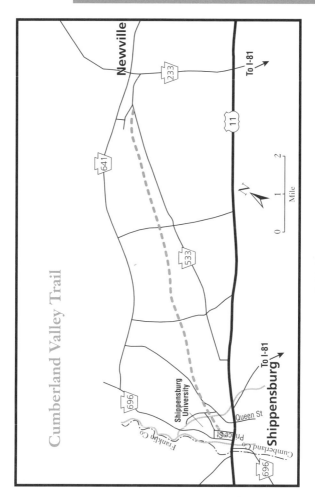

Location:	Cumberland County
Miles:	11
Endpoints:	Shippensburg to Newville
Surface:	Dirt, grass, original ballast (to be improved)
Contact:	Jack Conroy
	Cumberland Valley Rails-to-Trails Council
	PO Box 531
	Shippensburg, PA 17257
	717-530-1047
Equestrian	Diane Morrow
Contact:	717-352-7681

D & H Rail-Trail

In August 1829, the Delaware & Hudson Gravity Railroad conducted a trial test of the first steam locomotive to operate in the United States. Built in England, the "Stourbridge Lion" traveled an astonishing three miles from Honesdale to Seeleyville when its operators discovered it was too heavy for the track. By 1830, the 17 miles of the D&H Railroad constituted the vast majority of railroad mileage in the United States—23 whole miles!

From these small beginnings, shipping anthracite coal and lumber from Carbondale to Honesdale, the Delaware & Hudson became a successful mining and railroad company. By 1870, hard coal from the rich mines of the Lackawanna Valley was rolling north out of Carbondale to points all over the northeastern United States and Canada on the D&H line that became the trail.

Paralleling the Lackawanna River and the O&W Road Trail (see page 80) for several miles, the D&H Rail-Trail offers scenic vistas of the river corridor: waterfalls, clear pools and rhododendron-lined banks. Currently usable by hikers, mountain bikers, snowmobilers, and cross-country skiers, the D&H Rail-Trail will be a vital resource for the communities of northeastern Pennsylvania.

To reach Simpson, take I-81 to Exit 57, then Route 6 to Carbondale. After the town of Carbondale, turn left onto Route 171. Continue about one mile, park on right side of viaduct in Simpson. Take the O&W Trail for one mile, where it accesses the D&H to the west.

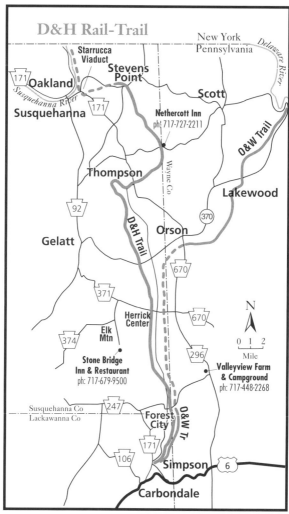

D&H Rail-Trail

Location:	Lackawanna, Wayne and Susquehanna Counties
Miles:	32
Endpoints:	Simpson to Stevens Point
Surface:	Cinder, original ballast (to be resurfaced)
Contact:	Lynn Conrad
	Rail-Trail Council of N.E. Pennsylvania
	PO Box 123
	Forest City, PA 18421-0123
	717-785-7245

Eliza Furnace Trail

Laughlin and Company built two of the famous Eliza Furnaces in 1861. The famous Jones and Laughlin Steel Company was formed in 1902 when Benjamin Franklin Jones, owner of an interest in the American Iron Works and Laughlin Steel Company merged with Laughlin Steel. In keeping with Victorian tradition, furnaces were named after women because they were considered fickle and temperamental. One of Jones' granddaughters was named Eliza. The Jones and Laughlin Steel Company at its peak occupied over 750 acres and seven miles of riverfront along the Ohio and Monogahela River and employed 30,000 at its facilities. The Hot Metal Bridge carried iron by rail from the Eliza furnaces to the Southside where finished steel was produced and shipped. As the Big Steel Industry changed, the Eliza furnaces were shut down on June 22, 1979. They were replaced by two electric furnaces on the Southside. In 1983, "Anna" the last of the Eliza furnaces was demolished. Today the Pittsburgh High Technology Park sits were the furnaces were once located.

The first phase of the trail extends from the First Avenue Parking Lot to Swinburne Street and is 2.5 miles long. Phase Two will extend the trail through Panther Hollow and up to Schenley Park and Oakland. The trail is being constructed by the City of Pittsburgh's Department of Public Works. Highlights along the trail include spectacular views of the Monongahela River, the Pittsburgh Technology Center, and the Southside and the Southside Slopes neighborhoods.

To access the trail from downtown Pittsburgh, take 2nd Avenue and make a left onto Swinburne Street. Parking is available at Swineburne Street and 2nd Avenue.

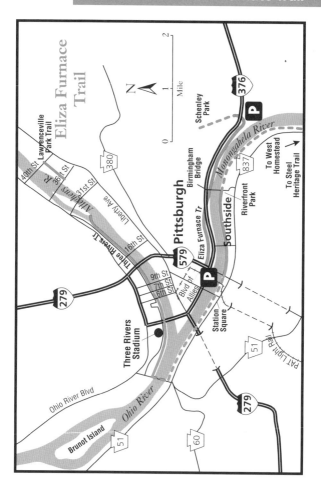

Location:	Allegheny County
Miles:	2.5 miles
Endpoints:	First Ave. Parking Lot to Swinburne St.
Surface:	10 foot wide asphalt path with crushed limestone on either side
Contact:	Office of the Mayor
	414 Grant Street
	Room 512, City County Building
	Pittsburgh, PA 15219
	412-255-2626

Endless Mountain Riding Trail

It pays to have friends in high places, or so the story goes for the Endless Mountain Trail. A retired judge living in Montrose in 1943 had such a friend. The judge, a former World War I cavalryman, was involved in a local riding club and happened to have a very good friend who worked for the Delaware, Lackawanna & Western Railroad. When the Montrose Branch was abandoned in 1944, the judge's friend sold it to him for one dollar, creating a trail for the riding club and one of the nation's first rail-trails. After enjoying the trail for many years, the original members of the club gave the right-of-way to the Bridgewater Riding Club, which has continued the trail's tradition.

Heavily forested for much of its length, this very rugged trail begins near a golf course and passes by many farms and rural homes. Along the way, you will enjoy a 60-foot waterfall, intact railroad ties alongside the trail, and an old railroad depot. You may also hear or see a pileated woodpecker if you're lucky! Although perfect for horseback riding, the trail is also used for mountain biking and hiking, and is home to a 10k race every July 4th.

The trail starts behind the Humane Society facility in Montrose. Take Route 706 (Grow Avenue) in Montrose to the Society and park there.

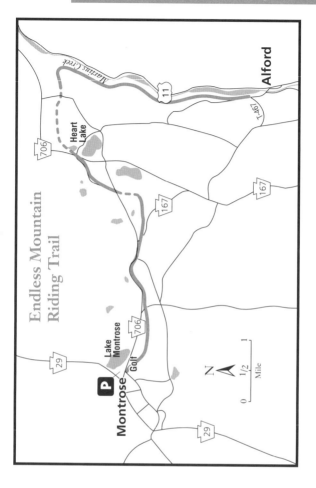

Location: Susquehanna County
Miles: 14
Endpoints: Alford to Montrose
Surface: Original ballast
Contact: Roy Brown
    Bridgewater Riding Club
    RR 4
    Montrose, PA 18801
    717-278-9406

43

Ernst Bike Trail

The Meadville-Linesville Railroad was built from 1880-1892 by a group of Meadville entrepreneurs to gain access to the Pennsylvania Railroad at Linesville. Despite the involvement of some of Meadville's best-known citizens, the railroad did not flourish.

In 1891, the Bessemer & Lake Erie Railroad Company leased the right-of-way and for a time its most profitable use was as a passenger line, transporting visitors to Exposition Park (renamed Conneaut Lake Park in 1920). With the rise of the automobile, passenger service declined and in 1934 rail service to the park was discontinued. The Bessemer abandoned the line in 1976. In 1996, Calvin Ernst, the right-of-way's owner, donated the property to French Creek Recreational Trails and the Ernst Bike Trail was born.

Traversing terrain with imprints of Ice Age glaciation, the trail passes through the lush bottom lands of French Creek Valley. With 66 species of fish and 27 species of mollusks, French Creek is Pennsylvania's most biologically diverse body of water. From the creek to the end of the trail's completed portion, the landscape is pastoral with varied environments of meadow and marsh, hardwood stands and hemlock thickets. The proposed segment from Route 19 to Conneaut Lake parallels Conneaut Marsh, an ancient river valley infield with glacial debris, and home to nesting bald eagles and migrating waterfowl.

The trail is currently accessed at its middle, located at the track crossing on Old Mercer Pike. The distance in either direction is approximately 2.5 miles.

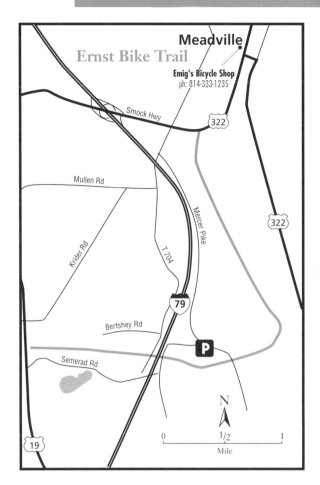

Location:	Crawford County
Miles:	5
Endpoints:	Meadville to Rt 19
Surface:	Crushed stone
Contact:	John Wallach
	French Creek Recreational Trails, Inc.
	c/o Community Health Services
	747 Terrace Street
	Meadville, PA 16335
	814-333-2063

Five Star Trail

The Five Star Trail is a "Rail-with-Trail" located along the Southwest Pennsylvania Railroad corridor between Greensburg and Youngwood, in central Westmoreland County. This 6.6 mile trail begins at the Lynch Field Recreation complex, located off Route 119 North in Greensburg and travels south to the Westmoreland County Community College in Youngwood. It is a non-motorized recreational trail for walking, jogging, bicycling and cross country skiing, as well as an alternative transportation resource for residents of central Westmoreland county. Trail visitors may wish to stop in at Youngwood Trail Station, a small museum that focusses on local and railroad history.

The rail corridor was purchased from Conrail in 1995 by the Westmoreland County Industrial Development Corporation. The rail is operated by the Southwest Pennsylvania Railroad and provides frieght service through central Westmoreland County. The trail is being managed by the Five Star Trail Chapter of the Regional Trail Corporation. The name "Five Star" comes from the five municipalities that joined forces to construct and manage the trail: City of Greensburg, Hempfield Township, and the Boroughs of Youngwood, South Greensburg, and Southwest Greensburg.

Trail access and parking is available at the intersection of Route 119 and Huff Avenue in Youngwood and at the Lynch Field Recreation Complex off Route 119 N in Greensburg.

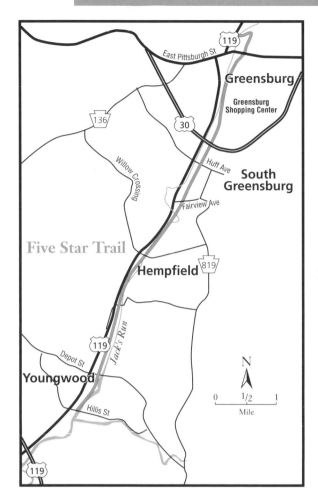

Location: Westmoreland County
Miles: 6.6
Endpoints: Greensburg to Youngwood
Surface: Crushed limestone and asphalt
Contact: Malcom N. Sias
    Five Star Trail Chapter
    R.R. #12, Box 203
    Greensburg, PA 15601
    724-830-3962

Forks Township Recreation Trail

Traveling as it does through cornfields and woodlands, the Forks Township Recreation Trail feels like a quiet country lane. The trail meanders past old stone fencing and rocky outcrops, and passes high above the Delaware River. It's a welcome respite for local workers, who often take their lunch breaks along its quiet pathway.

Built by the Lehigh & New England Railroad, the corridor connected at Martins Creek with the Delaware, Lackawanna & Western Railroad. The DL&W was one of northeastern Pennsylvania largest railroads and its network of railroad corridors forms the backbone of rail-trail construction in this area of the state.

Take Exit 6 (13th Street) from Route 22 in Easton and turn left at stoplight onto 13th Street. At the next traffic light (Bushkill Drive) turn left. After three miles, turn right onto Newlins Road West and then left at Sullivan Trail. Make a quick right turn back onto Newlins Road West. At the intersection with Broadway, turn right and follow Broadway .2 miles to the trailhead.

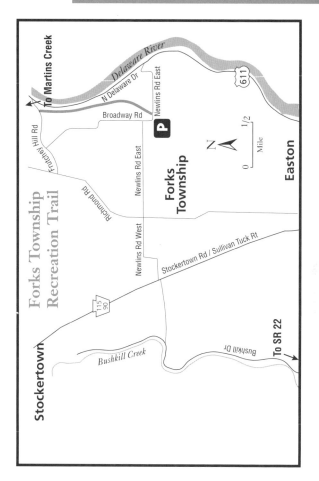

Location: Northampton County
Miles: 1.5
Endpoints: Uhlers Station to Frutchey Hill Road
Surface: Asphalt
Contact: Forks Township
1606 Sullivan Trail
Easton, PA 18040
610-252-0785

Ghost Town Trail

Five different railroads operated in the Blacklick Valley, most notably the Cambria & Indiana (originally the Blacklick and Yellow Creek, a logging railroad) and the Pennsylvania Railroad's Blacklick Secondary, the two lines that have become the Ghost Town Trail.

The lines once served eight coal mining towns, a lumbering town and mill, and three iron furnaces in the valley. Now all that marks this once-bustling industrial area are a few buildings and a lot of foundations.

Along the way, you'll pass woodlands and parallel Blacklick Creek. You'll find railroad bridges and creeks stocked with trout, abandoned mining towns, and Eliza Iron Furnace, which is one of Pennsylvania's best preserved iron furnaces and a national historic site. You'll traverse state game land—home to a variety of wildlife, including bear, turkey, deer, and songbirds.

Go eastbound on US22 from Blairsville to its intersection with US119. For the westernmost (Dilltown) trailhead, stay east on 22 for 11.6 miles to PA403. Turn left off the exist and continue 1.4 miles to the trailhead. Parking is on the left shortly after 403 crosses the creek. For the Nanty Glo (easternmost) trailhead, stay on 22 eastbound for 20 miles to PA271. Turn left on 271 and continue 1.5 miles to Nanty Glo. Just after crossing South Branch Blacklick Creek, turn left at the Nanty Glo Fire Station and follow the river about a block to the trailhead. Park at the far end of the lot, between the municipal building and firestation.

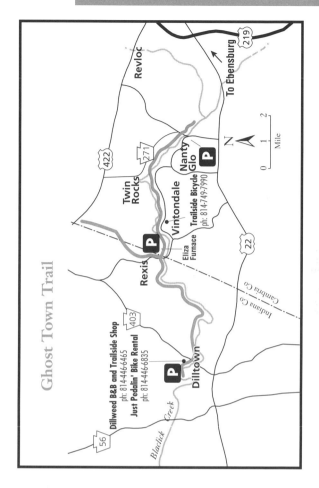

Location: Cambria and Indiana Counties
Miles: 16
Endpoints: Nanty Glo to Dilltown
Surface: Crushed limestone
Contact: Indiana County Parks
         Blue Spruce Park Rd
         Indiana, PA 15701
         724-463-8636

Great Shamokin Path

Built as the Rural Valley Railroad, the Great Shamokin Path is named after the path that once linked the Allegheny and Susquehanna Rivers and ran from Kittanning to Sunbury. The Rural Valley Railroad eventually wound up in the hands of the Baltimore and Ohio, which abandoned the Yatesboro to NuMine section in 1964.

The line was purchased in 1984 by the Cowanshannock Creek Watershed Association, a non-profit volunteer organization dedicated to improving the water quality of the creek. Acquisition funds for the trail came from the granting of a water main easement under the trail. This type of joint use is increasingly popular as a means of rail-trail development.

This mostly grass-covered trail climbs steadily through the Cowanshannock Creek Valley past the Devil's Washbasin, a 1.5 acre lake named for its dam across the creek to obtain water for steam engines - always smokey, steamy and eerie looking. The lake is stocked with fish and offers ice fishing and picnicking.

Near the trail's upper end, White Lake and its adjacent wetlands were created in 1988 to improve water quality in the creek which had deteriorated because of acid mine drainage.

Go east on PA85, just north of Kittanning off PA28/66 to Yatesboro. The Valley Village Store is at the west end of Yatesboro. Just east of the store before the turnoff to Yatesboro, an unmarked lot on the right provides parking for the westernmost trailhead. To reach the trailhead in NuMine, continue on PA85 about 3 miles east from Yatesboro. Turn right at the intersection where a left turn leads to NuMine. Immediately cross Cowanshannock Creek, turn right between the ballfield and the creek. A gated trailhead is just ahead, or you may drive a little farther to the White Lake picnic area.

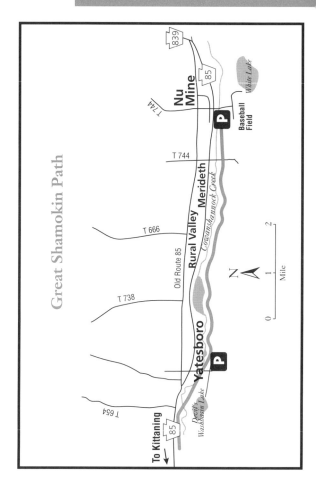

Location: Armstrong County
Miles: 4.5
Endpoints: Yatesboro to NuMine
Surface: Gravel, original ballast
Contact: Pam Meade
       Cowanshannock Creek Watershed Association
       PO Box 307
       Rural Valley, PA 16249
       724-783-6692

Indian Creek Valley Trail

The Indian Creek Valley Railroad (ICVRR) was built to Indian Head in 1906, and extended to Jones Mill, near Donegal, by the time it was finished in 1910. The ICVRR continued to operate until 1926, carrying passengers and freight to meet the Baltimore and Ohio Railroad (B&O) at the juncture of Indian Creek and the Youghiogheny River. The B&O bought the ICVRR and continued operating the main line until 1972, when it was completed abandoned. The Western Pennsylvania Conservancy then acquired the corridor and offered it to Saltlick Township, which opened the trail in 1989.

Perfect for hiking and mountain biking, the Indian Creek Valley Trail is a great escape from the crowds in the nearby Ohiopyle area. The right-of-way continues south to the Youghiogheny River and could one day be linked with the Youghiogheny River Trail.

Take the Pennsylvania Turnpike to the Donegal exit (exit 9), go east on PA 31, then south on 711/381. To Champion, follow 711/381 south 1.3 miles to SR1058 and turn left. The trailhead is about .25 mile down SR1058. For Indian Head, stay on 711/381 south for about 6 miles and turn left on SR1054. Just past Resh's store, turn left on Hull Street to a parking lot near the ballfield. The trailhead is on the opposite side of the ballfield from the creek along Hull Street.

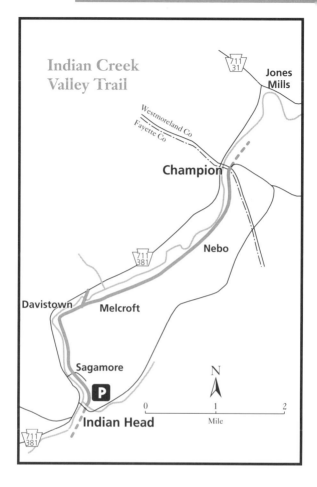

Indian Creek
Valley Trail

Jones
Mills

Westmoreland Co
Fayette Co

Champion

Nebo

Davistown   Melcroft

Sagamore

P

Indian Head

N

0   1   2
Mile

Location:	Fayette and Westmoreland Counties
Miles:	5
Endpoints:	Champion to Indian Head
Surface:	Crushed aggregate
Contact:	Saltlick Township
	PO Box 403
	Melcroft, PA 15462
	724-455-2866

Iron Horse Trail

This trail follows two abandoned railbeds, the Path Valley Railroad and the Perry Lumber Company Railroad. The Path Valley Railroad was never completed due to financial and construction problems. Originally, it was going to be an extension for the Newport and Shermans Valley Railroad and would end in Hancock, Maryland. After the grade was constructed to New Germantown, builders decided it would not be possible to tunnel through Conococheague Mountain so the venture was abandoned.

The Perry Lumber Company purchased a Climax locomotive in 1901 to remove 19,000 acres of timber from western Perry County. When the company disbanded in 1906, the track and land were sold to the Commonwealth, becoming one of the first large purchases for the Tuscarora State Forest.

Located in Tuscarora State Forest, this 10-mile trail was constructed in 1981 by the US Youth Conservation Corps, working with the Department of Environmental Resources' Bureau of Forestry.

Unlike some rail-trails, the Iron Horse Trail has some moderate climbs and requires good hiking boots. There are two different sections of the trail. The one on the north side of PA Route 274 follows the Path Valley Railroad grade; the one on the south side follows the Perry Lumber Company Railroad.

Big Spring State Park and its trailhead are located on PA274 near the Perry/Franklin County line. A second trailhead is located two miles southwest of New Germantown on Route 274.

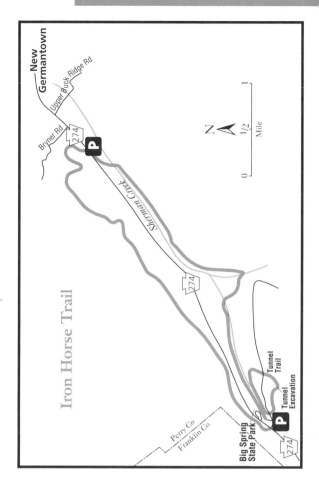

Location:	Perry County
Miles:	10
Endpoints:	Big Spring State Park to New Germantown
Surface:	Dirt, original ballast
Contact:	Bureau of Forestry
	RD 1, Box 42A
	Blain, PA 17006
	717-536-3191

Ironton Rail-Trail

In 1882, the Ironton Railroad was purchased from the Lehigh Valley Railroad by the Thomas Iron Works Company to transport the tons of coal, iron ore, and limestone that fueled the nation's most powerful blast furnace. In that same year, David Thomas founded the village of Hokendauqua to house his employees. In 1996, Whitehall Township purchased the corridor from Conrail to create the Ironton Rail-Trail. The Borough of Coplay and North Whitehall Township are buying their respective sections.

Boasting no fewer than 10 sites of historic significance, the former Ironton Railroad corridor is awash with the history of the Lehigh Valley. The trail cuts through the 110-acre Whitehall Parkway, preserving the remains of the limestone and cement industry that first brought wealth and recognition to the region. The corridor then splits as it approaches the Borough of Coplay, providing, when complete, a unique 6.25-mile loop through the Borough and the village of Hokendauqua along the Lehigh River, before rejoining the main corridor for the ride back to the village of Ironton.

The trail may be accessed at many points along its length. Parking is presently available in Whitehall Parkway. From Route 22E, take the exit for Route 145N (MacArthur Road). Follow MacArthur Road through several traffic lights to Chestnut Street. Turn left onto Chestnut Street and park behind the barn at Whitehall Parkway. The trail begins just down Chestnut Street from the parking lot.

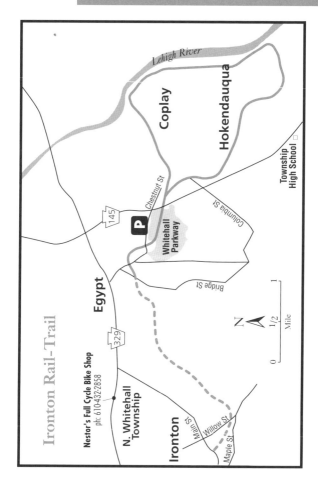

Location:	Lehigh County
Miles:	9
Endpoints:	Whitehall Township
Surface:	Crushed stone and asphalt
Contact:	Scott J. Cope
	Whitehall Township
	Bureau of Recreation
	3219 MacArthur Road
	Whitehall, PA 18052
	610-437-5524

Jim Mayer Riverswalk

The late Jim Mayer was a Johnstown area conservationist whose efforts to preserve natural resources have been incorporated into development of this trail. The land on which the trail is built was part of the Johnstown and Stonycreek Railroad. The Glosser Family Foundation subsequently bought the land from the former railroad and donated it to the Cambria County Transit Authority to be preserved. This 1.2-mile trail was dedicated on May 13, 1993 and provides recreation for local residents as well as travelers passing through the area.

The Jim Mayer Riverswalk Trail is nestled in the heart of Johnstown. As this beautiful trail winds along the Stonycreek River, it offers the tranquillity of the Pennsylvania highlands amidst a metropolitan setting. The introduction of birdhouses along the trail has added to the existing natural habitat for wildlife, including deer.

To reach the trail, take PA403 (Central Avenue) in Johnstown south to Bridge Street in the Moxham District of the City. The trailhead is located on the left.

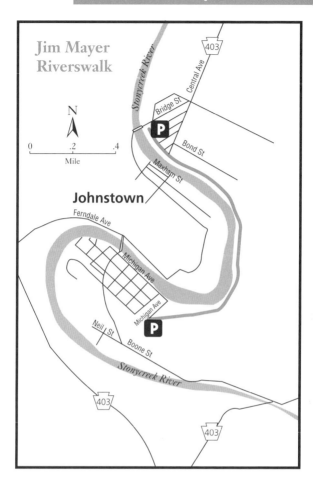

Location:	Cambria County
Miles:	1.2
Endpoints:	Moxham/Bridge Street to Riverside/Michigan Avenue (Johnstown)
Surface:	Packed gravel
Contact:	Rose Lucey-Noll Cambria County Transit Authority 726 Central Avenue Johnstown, PA 15902 814-535-5526

Kinzua Bridge Trail

The Kinzua railroad bridge was the highest railroad bridge in the world when it was built in 1882. Originally made of iron, the bridge is 301 feet high and spans the Kinzua Creek Valley for 2,053 feet. In 1890, the entire structure had to be rebuilt to accommodate heavier trains. It took more than 100 men working 10 hours a day exactly 105 days to complete a new 6.5 million pound steel structure. It is now the second highest railroad bridge in the country and the fourth highest in the world.

The Erie Railroad abandoned the bridge in 1959 and the line was sold for scrap to the Kovalchick Company, which then donated the bridge to the state. In 1970, the Kinzua State Park opened and in 1977 the Kinzua Bridge was placed on the National Register of Historic Civil Engineering Landmarks. Today, the Knox, Kane and Kinzua Railroad offers excursion rides over the bridge starting from Marienville or Kane.

Adventure awaits you on the Kinzua Bridge Trail. You'll follow the abandoned Erie Railroad line through a small portion of the 316-acre Kinzua Bridge State Park. After enjoying the woodlands and wildlife along the trail, you'll come to the highlight of your trip, the Kinzua railroad bridge. The faint of heart might want to stay on the overlook rather than walking out onto the bridge itself. For non-acrophobics, the bridge is equipped with a deck and railings so visitors can walk its full 2,053-foot length. You're guaranteed to be impressed by the scenery and amazing engineering of the second highest railroad bridge in the country.

Kinzua Bridge State Park is located 4 miles north of US Route 6 in Mt. Jewett on SR3011.

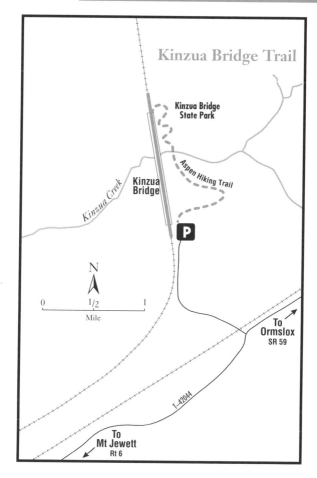

Location:	McKean County
Miles:	1.0
Endpoints:	Kinzua Bridge State Park
Surface:	Wooden planks
Contact:	Kinzua Bridge State Park
	c/o Bendigo State Park
	PO Box A
	Johnsonburg, PA 15845
	814-965-2646
	www.dcnr.state.pa.us

Lackawanna River Heritage Trail

The Lackawanna River Heritage Trail is being developed by the Lackawana Heritage Valley Authority along 40 miles of the Lackawanna River located near Scranton, Pennsylvania. The trail follows abandoned sections of the Central Railroad of New Jersey and the former New York Ontario and Western Railway (NYO & W) between Scranton and Carbondale.

The Central New Jersey Rail Road (CNJRR) was part of the Lehigh Coal and Navigation system which operated the coal mine's railroads and canals to transport anthracite coal from the Lackawanna and Wyoming Valleys in Northeastern Pennsylvania to markets along the east coast. This portion of the CNJRR was abandoned after the floods of 1972. Additional sections of the Lackawanna River Heritage Trail are under development along the former New York Ontario and Western Railway (NYO & W) between Scranton and Carbondale. Several sections will be open in 1999-2000 and will provide linkages to the D&H and O&W Trails .

The 1.5 miles of Lackawanna River Heritage Trail currently opened runs from 7th Avenue to Elm Street in Scranton. There are three parking areas to access this trail; at 7th Avenue near Lackawanna Avenue, at the William Schmidt Recreation Park on Broadway Street and at Elm Street off South Washington Avenue. This section of trail has a variety of features of interest from Historic Sites to Class 'A' trout fisheries and brownfield sites of interest to the Industrial Archeologist.

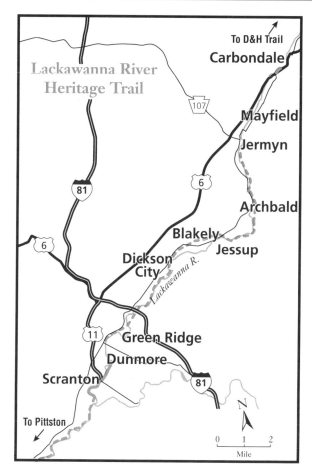

Lackawanna River Heritage Trail

Location:	Lackawanna County
Miles:	40 miles (1.5 miles complete)
Endpoints:	North Seventh Avenue to Elm Street, City of Scranton
Surface:	Crushed limestone on 1.5 mile developed section. Dirt and cinder on other areas.
Contact:	Lackawanna River Corridor Association 2006 North Main Avenue Scranton, PA 18508 717-347-6311
Contact:	Lackawanna Heritage Valley Authority 1300 Old Plank Road Mayfield, PA 18433 717-876-6188

Lambs Creek Bike & Hike Trail

When the Tioga-Hammond Lakes were created by the US Army Corps of Engineers, the abandoned Erie Lackawanna Railroad became a trail.

Originally the Erie Railroad Tioga Division, the line once ran as far as Hoytville. It was abandoned after the Hurricane Agnes flood of 1972.

The Lambs Creek Recreation Area is situated next to Tioga Lakes and provides a variety of recreation opportunities. The 3.7 mile trail travels along the Tioga River, with fishing for tiger muskie, bass, walleye, and channel catfish among the pleasures to be found.

Picnic sites, shelters, volleyball courts and horseshoe pits are also located nearby. One other feature not to be missed is the overlook on the rock outcrops which separate Tioga and Hammond Lakes.

Take Lambs Creek Road just west of Mansfield on Route 6 to the trailhead in the park. The trail may also be accessed behind the BiLo Supermarket on North Main Street (Business US 15) in Mansfield.

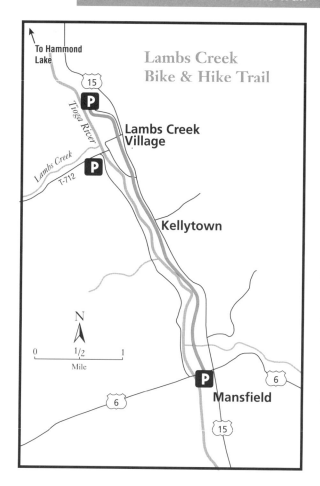

Lambs Creek
Bike & Hike Trail

To Hammond Lake

Tioga River

Lambs Creek

T-712

Lambs Creek Village

Kellytown

N

0   1/2   1
Mile

Mansfield

Location: Tioga County
Miles: 3.7
Endpoints: Lambs Creek Recreation Area
to Mansfield
Surface: Asphalt
Contact: US Army Corps of Engineers
RR 1, Box 65
Tioga, PA 16946-9733
717-835-5281

Lancaster Junction Trail

Originally the Reading & Columbia Railroad, this branch of the Reading Railroad was built to haul anthracite coal to Columbia where it was loaded into barges on the Susquehanna and Tidewater Canal for shipment to the port of Baltimore. The Reading also owned the canal and used it to compete directly with rival Pennsylvania Railroad for Baltimore coal traffic. After the canal ceased operation in 1894, the railroad became just another rural branch line. It was abandoned in 1985 and became a trail in 1987.

The Lancaster Junction Trail travels through meadows, past rich Lancaster farmland and along winding Chickies Creek. This trail is perfect for horseback riding, cross-country skiing, or jogging.

The southern trailhead near Landisville is found at the end of Champ Boulevard, just east of Spooky Nook Road and the Salunga exit of I-283. The trail may also be accessed just west of Lancaster Junction on Auction Road.

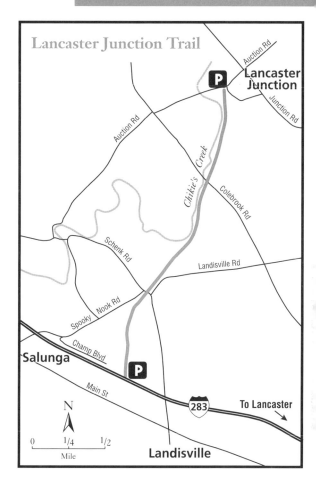

Lancaster Junction Trail

Location:	Lancaster County
Miles:	2.5
Endpoints:	Lancaster Junction to Landisville
Surface:	Cinder
Contact:	Lancaster County Parks & Recreation
	1050 Rockford Road
	Lancaster, PA 17602
	717-299-8215

Lehigh Gorge State Park Trail

This trail is located in the Lehigh Gorge State Park, an area best known for its whitewater rafting.

The trail was built along a rail line that was originally constructed by the Central Railroad of New Jersey. The line traversed the Lehigh Gorge to tap the anthracite coal fields in the Hazleton and Wilkes-Barre areas. With coal exhausted, other business could not sustain the Central Railroad, which made way for the Lehigh Valley Railroad in 1965. The Lehigh Valley Railroad then abandoned the line in 1972.

North of Jim Thorpe, the right-of-way parallels and active Conrail track for six miles. This rails-with-trails option is one of 37 similar joint-use ventures in the nation. The active track is used six to eight times daily; the trail accommodates approximately 30,000 trail users each year. There have never been any trail-track related accidents.

Spectacular scenery and roaring rapids await you in the Lehigh Gorge. Remember to bring your camera for this trail! You'll click the shutter more than a few times as you follow the Lehigh River along its rocky escarpments. If you would like to experience the river in a more personal way, there are also many opportunities for kayaking, canoeing, rafting, and fishing.

To reach the northern trailhead near White Haven, take Exit 40 from I-80 into White Haven Borough. The southern trailhead just outside of Jim Thorpe is located on Coalport Road, just north of PA903 in Jim Thorpe.

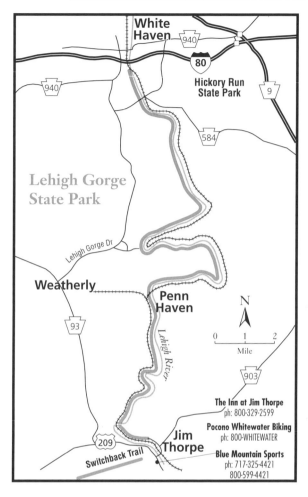

 on certain sections

Location:	Luzerne and Carbon Counties
Miles:	25
Endpoints:	White Haven to Jim Thorpe
Surface:	Cinder, crushed stone
Contact:	Lehigh Gorge State Park
	c/o Hickory Run State Park
	RR 1, Box 81
	White Haven, PA 18661
	717-443-0400
	www.dcnr.state.pa.us

LeTort Spring Run Nature Trail

James LeTort, the namesake for the stream and trail, was a noted pioneer who lived near the banks of LeTort Spring Run. Mr. LeTort acted as interpreter for the government when communicating with local Native Americans.

The South Mountain Iron Company built the railroad in about 1870 to run from Carlisle along LeTort Spring Run to Pine Grove Furnace. After 1891, the Reading Railroad operated the line, in use until the Hurricane Agnes flood in 1972. The LeTort Regional Authority purchased the right-of-way in 1974 and converted it into a 1.4-mile nature trail.

Known for its excellent trout fishing, LeTort Spring Run is considered a classic limestone stream and is the perfect companion for a trip along this trail. The clear water makes stalking fish easier for fishermen searching for a catch—please remember to be quiet when you see anglers at work!

Surrounding the trail is a mixture of deciduous trees, including oak, maple, and locust. Along the banks of the LeTort are many lowland marshes with cattails, marsh grasses, and a variety of animals, including muskrats, ducks, salamanders, and frogs.

Easiest access to the trail is found in LeTort Park, on East Pomfret Street in the Borough of Carlisle. From High Street, turn south on Spring Garden, then west onto Pomfret Street. The park is on the left. A second trailhead is located on Bonnybrook Road, just east of Route 34. Going south on Route 34, Lindsay Lane is a left turn, .7 miles past Exit 14 of I-81. Bonnybrook Road intersects with Lindsay Lane.

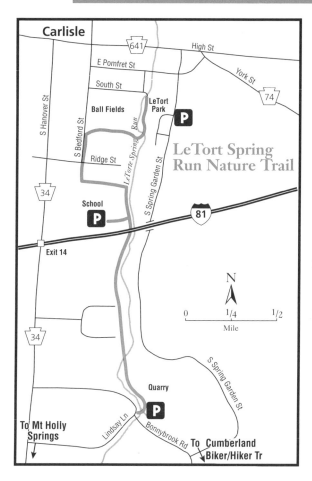

Location: Cumberland County
Miles: 1.4
Endpoints: Carlisle to South Middleton Township
Surface: Original ballast
Contact: Brian Fischbach
          LeTort Regional Authority
          415 Franklin Street
          Carlisle, PA 17013
          717-245-0508

Little Buffalo State Park Trail

The Little Buffalo State Park Trail is located in Little Buffalo State Park in Perry County. This trail has connections to 7 miles of hiking trails located within the State Park. Highlights alongside the trail include access to fishing along Holman Lake, a covered bridge over a Furnace Run (Creek), Shoaff's Grist Mill, and an original rail car "Way Car No. 12".

The Newport and Shermans Valley Railroad transversed Perry County hauling lumber, tanbark, freight, and passengers. The construction of the first 16 miles of the steam powered railroad only took about 6 months in 1890 at the cost of $7,900 per mile. By 1893, the Newport and Shermans Valley Railroad traveled another 14 miles from Loysville to New Germantown.

In 1913, it only cost 72 cents to ship 480 pounds of freight 25 miles from Newport to Blain. The Newport and Shermans Valley Railroad transported vital deliveries of tan bark to tanneries in Newport. Also it was popular passenger train with each town along the track having its own train station. The railway was last used in the early 1930's, when it succumbed to financial difficulties and changing times.

Little Buffalo State Park is comprised of 830 acres in scenic Perry County. Travel PA Route 34 and exit west between New Bloomfield and Newport. The rail-trail can be accessed at Shoaff's Mill and the Main Picnicking Area end of Little Buffalo State Park. Parking is available at both locations.

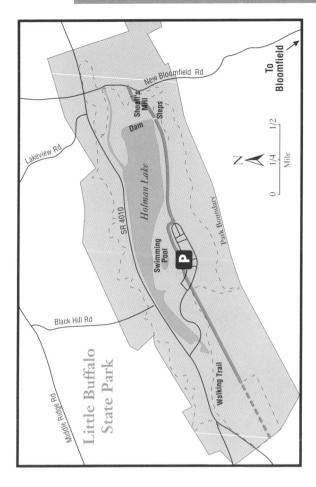

Location:	Perry County
Miles:	2.5 miles
Endpoints:	Shoeff's Mill to the Western Border of Little Buffalo State Park
Surface:	Dirt/Gravel
Contact:	Little Buffalo State Park
	RD 2 Box 256A
	Newport, PA 17074-9428
	717-567-9255
	www.dcnr.state.pa.us

Lower Trail

The Lower (rhymes with "flower") Trail follows the corridor of the old Pennsylvania canal. Built in the 1830s, the canal was a continuous system of waterways and railroads from Philadelphia to Pittsburgh.

As improvements were made to locomotives, the "iron horse" soon proved superior to mule-towed canal boats, and by the 1850s the Pennsylvania Railroad had replaced the slow and inefficient canal system.

In 1879, a railroad known as the Petersburg Branch of the PRR was built along the corridor. The line continued to operate until 1979 but was officially abandoned in 1982. In 1990, the line was purchased by the local rails-to-trails group from a donation made by Attorney T. Dean Lower.

Following the Frankstown Branch of the Juniata River, the Lower Trail features beautiful scenery through forest and farmland as well as portions of canal locks, channels and lock tender house remnants. The trail also passes the Mt. Etna Furnace, where iron ore was smelted.

From Hollidaysburg, go east on US22, 18.6 miles east from its intersection with PA36. Turn left on SR4014 toward Alfarata and then .4 miles to trailhead parking. For Williamsburg, the southernmost trailhead, follow US22 9.1 miles east from PA SR 36. Turn right on PA SR 866 and proceed into Williamsburg, where it becomes First Street. Stay on First Street when SR 866 turns right, and go two blocks farther to trailhead parking at the intersection of First and Liberty Streets.

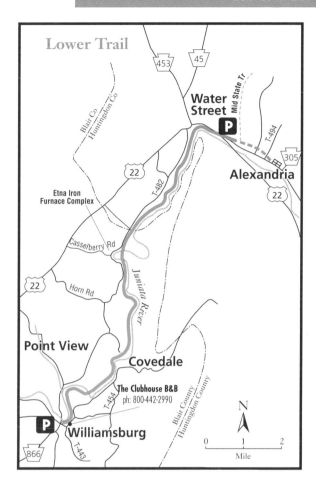

Lower Trail

Location:	Blair and Huntingdon Counties
Miles:	11
Endpoints:	Alexandria to Williamsburg
Surface:	Crushed limestone
Contact:	Jennifer Barefoot
	Rails-to-Trails of Central Pennsylvania
	PO Box 529
	Hollidaysburg, PA 16648
	814-832-2400

Lycoming Creek Bikeway

Named "Legani Hanne" or "sandy creek" by the Delaware tribe, Lycoming Creek and its adjacent rail corridor have a significant history. Hundreds of years ago, these Native Americans developed a long foot trail along Lycoming Creek, which was known first as the Shesheguin Trail and later as Culbertson's Path. This trail spanned from Onondago, New York to the Carolinas.

In 1839, the first railroad in Lycoming County was constructed along a portion of the trail from Williamsport to Ralston. The railroad was later extended to Elmira, New York. The railroad and creek were heavily used to transport iron ore, coal and lumber from mines, grist mills and sawmills north of Williamsport, which was the lumber capital of the world in the late 19th century. The railroad even transported Confederate prisoners to a Union camp in Elmira during the Civil War.

Shortly after the Hurricane Agnes flood of 1972, the Penn Central Railroad Elmira Branch was abandoned by Conrail. The current bikeway built in 1991 along sections of this historic corridor, and also shares several well-marked streets in a residential area.

Following Lycoming Creek, and providing connections to the 11-mile bikeway system in the Williamsport Urbanized Area, the trail passes Carl E. Stotz Memorial Park with its monument to Mr. Stotz, the founder of Little League Baseball. Eventually the trail comes to a wooden pedestrian bridge crossing Lycoming Creek. The journey ends about a mile later at the Heshbon Recreation Park. Local efforts to continue the bikeway northward along the railroad are underway.

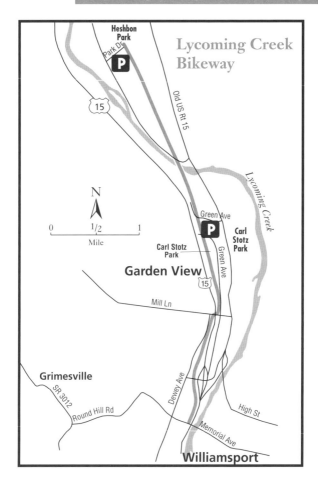

Location:	Lycoming County
Miles:	3.3
Endpoints:	Heshbon Park to Memorial Avenue, Williamsport
Surface:	Asphalt
Contact:	Mark Murawski
	Lycoming County Planning Commission
	48 West Third Street
	Williamsport, PA 17701
	717-320-2138

Middle Creek Trail

In June 1914, the Ephrata and Lebanon Street Railway Company completed construction of a 22.7-mile trolley line between the towns of Ephrata and Lebanon. Passing through the nine small towns, the trip took an hour and a half.

All that remains of the line is the one-mile Middle Creek Trail, located on State Game Lands 46 in Lancaster County. Acting as the eastern side of a triangle formed with the Elders Run Trail and the 130-mile Horseshoe Trail, the Middle Creek Trail is contained within the Middle Creek Wildlife Management Area.

Encompassing 5,000 acres of protected habitat, the Management Area is seasonal home to thousands of migrating ducks, swans, and Canada Geese, as well as the year-round host to a bevy of pheasant, quail, ruffed grouse, and deer. Middle Creek also offers an informative visitors center and interpretive trails, including a Braille trail for the visually impaired.

To reach Middle Creek, take I-78 to exit 3 and proceed south on PA501 to Schaefferstown. Go east on Route 897 to Kleinfeltersville. Turn right on Hopeland Road to the Wildlife Management Area. To hike a downhill return trip, continue on Hopeland Road to Mountain Spring Road and turn right. Park in lot for State Gamelands on the right; follow Elders Run Trail a few hundred feet to Middle Creek Trail.

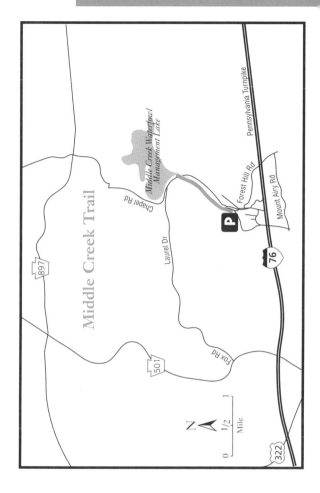

Location:	Lancaster County
Miles:	1
Endpoints:	Within management area
Surface:	Dirt, grass
Contact:	Middle Creek Wildlife Management Area PO Box 820 Newmanstown, PA 17073 717-733-1512

Montour Trail

The Montour Railroad was built in 1877 and eventually linked the Pittsburgh and Lake Erie Railroad with more than 30 coal mines. Forming a semi-circle around the city of Pittsburgh, the Montour also connected other railroads, including the Pennsylvania, the Pittsburgh & West Virginia, the Baltimore & Ohio, and the Union.

When completed, the Montour Trail's 55 miles will connect the Ohio and Monongahela Rivers, crossing numerous creeks and highways on a variety of bridges, including one almost 1,000 feet long, and three tunnels.

The main historical feature on the Cecil segment of the trail is the 620-foot National Tunnel, which passes under Klinger Road. This unusual tunnel is built on a curve and you will not be able to see one portal while standing at the other.

In winter, locals refer to this as the "National Cave" because of the icy stalactites that form in the tunnel. Many of these icicles reach halfway to the tunnel floor! Because of this phenomenon, the trail in the tunnel is surfaced with a coarse aggregate stone, which allows water to pass easily through to the french drains along the south side of the tunnel.

To reach the trailhead at Groveton, take I-79 north to Exit 17, PA51. Exit northbound on 51. PA51 crosses Montour Run on a high bridge within .5 mile. Just after the bridge, make a sharp right onto Montour Road. A small sign for the trail is located at the intersection. Go .1 mile on Montour Road to parking under the PA51 bridge.

To reach the trail's Cecil segment, take Exit 11 (Bridgeville) from I-79 and go west on PA50 6.7 miles to the Cecil Township Park in Venice. On the eastern end, take I-79 to the Hendersonville Exit (Exit 10A) and turn left to Hendersonville. Follow the signs .5 mile to SR1009, turn left and go .5 mile to the Hendersonville trailhead. Turn left at the Hendersonville shops, just before a now missing railroad bridge.

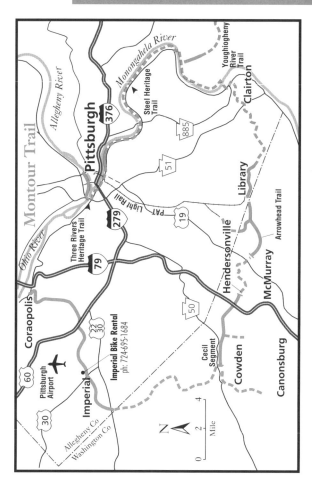

 on certain sections

Location:	Washington and Allegheny Counties
Miles:	Three segments of 11.5, 5.7 and 3 miles
Endpoints:	Coraopolis (Groveton) to Champion; Venice (Cecil Park) to Hendersonville; McDonald (Robinson Township) to Quicksilver
Surface:	Crushed limestone
Contact:	Montour Trail Council
	PO Box 11866
	Pittsburgh, PA 15228-0866
	412-831-2030
	www.atatrail.org

O & W Trail

Built in the 1880s to transport coal mined from the Lackawanna Valley's rich anthracite deposits, the New York, Ontario & Western's Scranton Division was just one part of a network of rails and canals connecting the Wyoming Valley to the East Coast.

By the 1940s, the demand for anthracite coal had declined, and the rails that once transported this vital energy source were slowly abandoned. When it was abandoned in 1957, the NYO&W was the largest railroad to be abandoned in the United States.

Along the trail, you will see beautiful views of the upper Lackawanna River, Shehawken Creek, Stillwater Cliffs, Stillwater Reservoir, and Stoneface. There are also lakes, wetlands, woodlands, and small communities that offer a variety of recreational activities.

The Delaware & Hudson (D&H) Trail (see page 104) parallels the O&W Road Trail for much of its length. The Rail-Trail Council of Northeastern Pennsylvania will be developing the D&H, using the O&W for loop trails, but with little improvements other than grading.

To reach Simpson, take I-81 to Exit 57, then Route 6 to Carbondale. After the town of Carbondale, turn left onto Route 171. Continue about one mile, park on right side of viaduct in Simpson. Enter the O&W along Homestead Street.

The northern 13 miles of the trail to the Delaware River is owned by Preston and Buckingham Townships. To access this section of the trail, take PA370 to Lakewood. The corridor is readily apparent, at the train station in the center of town.

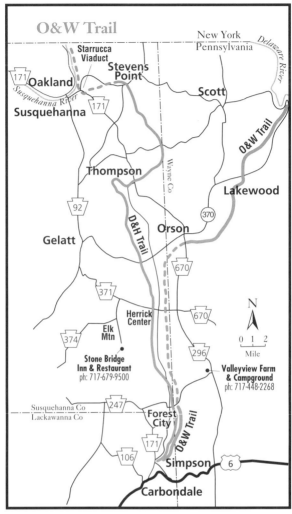

O&W Trail

Location:	Lackawanna, Wayne and Susquehanna Co.
Miles:	13 complete, 8 under construction
Endpoints:	Simpson to Stillwater
Surface:	Cinder, original ballast
Contact:	Lynn Conrad
	Rail-Trail Council of NE Pennsylvania
	PO Box 123
	Forest City, PA 18421-0123
	717-785-7245

Oil Creek State Park Trail

The Titusville and Petroleum Center Railroad had one major purpose when it was built in 1863—to transport oil. Oil was discovered in Oil Creek Valley in 1859 by Colonel Edward Drake and William Smith. Almost overnight, towns such as Titusville, Miller Farm, Pioneer, and Petroleum Center blossomed as opportunists rushed to get rich from the "Great Oil Dorado."

The oil boom ended in 1871 almost as quickly as it began. When the once-boisterous towns died away, the railroad hung on. Through a series of mergers, it became part of the Pennsylvania Railroad system in 1900 and was abandoned in 1945.

Few reminders of the thousands of people who once occupied the Oil Creek Valley remain. Today, the valley is home to hemlocks, beaver ponds, trout streams and waterfalls. The only evidence of the intense oil drilling that once went on here is the occasional well head.

Oil Creek State Park has 36 miles of hiking trails with camping shelters; 20 miles of cross-country ski trails; picnicking, canoeing, fishing, and bicycle rentals. The Oil Creek & Titusville excursion train runs through the park.

For the south trailhead, take the Route 8 bypass north around Oil City and continue 3.5 miles to the turnoff for Petroleum Center just after Route 8 crosses Oil Creek. Turn right on SR1007 and continue 3.1 miles to the junction of SR1007 and SR1004. Turn right on SR1004 and cross Oil Creek. Parking is just ahead on the left. For the northern trailhead at Drake Well Museum, again take the Route 8 bypass around Oil City, but proceed 14 miles north to the stop light at Bloss Street. Turn right and go just under a mile to parking on the right.

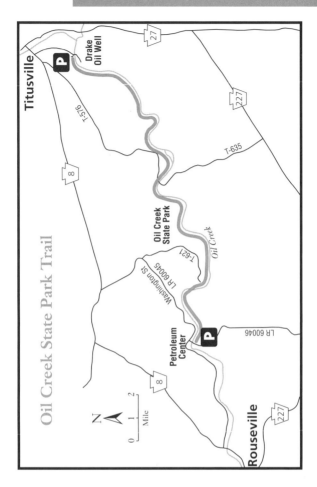

Oil Creek State Park Trail

Location:	Venango County				

Location: Venango County
Miles: 9.7
Endpoints: Petroleum Center to Drake Well Museum
Surface: Asphalt
Contact: Oil Creek State Park
RR 1, Box 207
Oil City, PA 16301
814-676-5915
www.dcnr.state.pa.us

Old Railroad Trail

The Wilkes-Barre & Eastern Railroad, built in 1893, ran for 62 mountainous miles between Wilkes-Barre and Stroudsburg. It operated as a branch of the Erie Railroad, but was never very successful. After suffering damage in the flood of 1936, the hapless line was abandoned in 1939.

Located near Big Pocono State Park, the trail opened in 1954, and connects with trails in the State Game Lands and Camelback ski resort.

Offering a variety of terrain and wildlife, including black bear, deer, fox, turkey, and ruffed grouse (the Pennsylvania state bird), the four trails available in Big Pocono State Park include the Old Railroad Trail (blazed blue), the South Trail (yellow), the North Trail (red), and the Indian Trail (orange). Combined, these trails provide ten miles for hiking, biking, and horseback riding.

The Old Railroad Trail begins near the park entrance and curves around the park boundary. Perfect for horseback riding or a leisurely stroll, the trail is smooth and gentle.

For those wishing a rougher, steeper climb into the summit of Camelback Mountain, turn onto the Indian Trail. At the summit, you will view areas of eastern Pennsylvania, and on a clear day you may even see New Jersey. Other highlights of the park include a nature museum, picnic areas, a scenic drive and a restaurant.

To reach the trail, take exit 45 from I-80 and head south on PA715. Turn right onto Railroad Avenue and follow it approximately one mile to the trailhead, which is on the right.

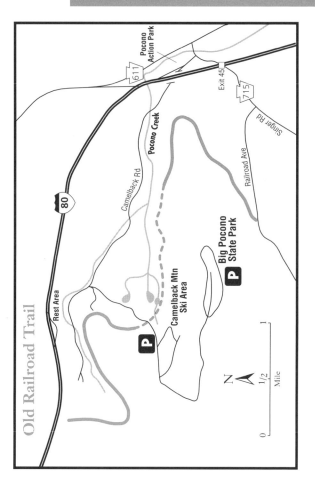

Location: Monroe County
Miles: 4
Endpoints: Big Pocono State Park to Crescent Lake
Surface: Crushed stone
Contact: Big Pocono State Park
PO Box 387
Tobyhanna, PA 18466
717-894-8336
www.dcnr.state.pa

Old Salem Trail

Originally part of the Clarion Secondary, a branch of the New York Central Railroad, the line was built to haul coal from the mines around Brookville to the Lake Erie port of Ashtabula. When the coal played out, the Clarion Secondary, like so many other coal-hauling railroads in Pennsylvania, was abandoned by Conrail in 1988.

The trail meanders through meadow, farmland and forest. It passes by a sylvan wetland, and the trail's wide corridor is reminiscent of a quiet country lane.

From I-79, take Route 358w toward Greenville about 8 miles. Turn right on Methodist Road (Campbell's Trail & Turf). Follow Methodist Road about a mile downhill and veer right. The trailhead is on left just past the Greenville Auction building.

DID YOU KNOW?

❏ There are more than 7,300 members of the Pennsylvania Field Office of Rails-to-Trails Conservancy working to make a statewide network of public trails!

❏ If you're not already a member, it's easy to join—just fill out the membership application at the end of this book.

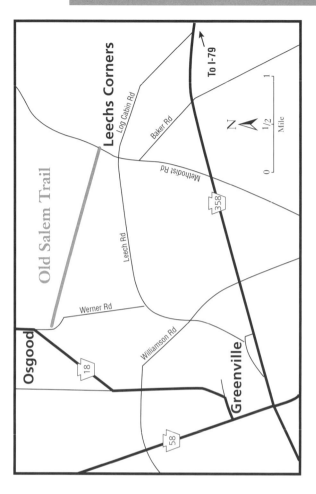

Location: Mercer County
Miles: 2.5
Endpoints: Salem Township to Osgood
Surface: Dirt, crushed stone
Contact: Sheryl Peterson
Mercer County Rails-to-Trails
681 North Neshannock Road
Hermitage, PA 16148
724-981-4489

Penns Creek Path

Part of the Mid-State Trail, a cross-country hiking trail that traverses four state forests and eight natural areas in the ridge and valley region of central Pennsylvania.

The main trail parallels the route of the old Penns Creek Indian Path and follows along the border of Huntingdon and Centre counties for more than 166 miles. The rail-trail section follows the abandoned railroad located in Poe Paddy State Park. Built in 1879, it linked all the small timber railroads that ran through the mountain valleys. Poe Paddy is located on the site of Poe Mills, a prosperous by short-lived lumber town of the 1880's and 1890s. There was also an excursion train that looped from Milroy to Poe Paddy in the 1900s. The railroad was abandoned in 1970.

There is much rugged beauty in this mountain valley. You might want to explore the Paddy Mountain Railroad Tunnel following Penns Creek upstream. You'll find excellent trout fishing in Penns Creek, which is nationally known for its green drake hatch in late May or early June. And there are plenty of picnic and camping areas to enjoy.

Poe Paddy State Park is located at the confluence of Big Poe Creek and Penns Creek, four miles east of Poe Valley State Park on the gravel Big Poe Road. Poe Valley State Park is located 1.5 miles east of Potters Mills on US 322, near the top of Seven Mountains Scenic Area. Follow marked State Forest roads for 10 miles to Poe Valley. The roads leading to the park are not entirely paved.

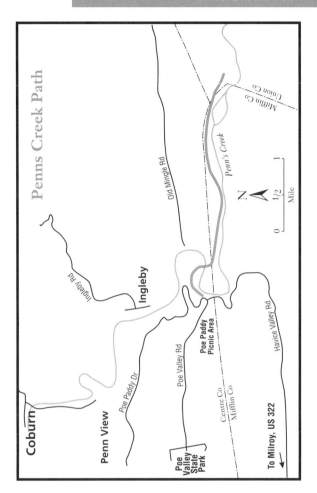

 on certain sections

Location:	Centre, Mifflin and Snyder Counties
Miles:	3.6
Endpoints:	Poe Paddy State Park to Cherry Run
Surface:	Original ballast
Contact:	Thomas T. Thwaites
	Mid State Trail Association
	PO Box 167
	Boalsburg, PA 16827
	814-237-7703

Pine Creek Trail

The Jersey Shore, Pine Creek & Buffalo Railroad began in 1883 by carrying timber to the sawmills in Tiadaghton, Cammal, and Slate Run, located along the floor of Pine Creek Gorge. The railroad also transported coal north to New York State and by 1896 was carrying seven million tons of freight and three passenger trains on daily runs between Wellsboro Junction and Williamsport.

The railroad changed hands a few times, becoming the Fallbrook Railroad, a branch of the New York Central Railroad, and the Penn Central before it was taken over by Conrail. The last freight train passed through the gorge on October 7, 1988, ending more than a century of service.

One of the most spectacular natural areas in the Commonwealth, the Pine Creek Gorge is often referred to as the Grand Canyon of Pennsylvania. It was recognized as a National Natural Landmark in 1969.

With 20 miles of developed trail, the corridor hugs Pine Creek for 62 miles, providing access to whitewater rafting and canoeing in the Spring, and great views of dramatic rock outcrops and numerous waterfalls. You may be lucky enough to see an eagle, osprey, or coyote, or catch a glimpse of a deer, wild turkey, heron, hawk, or one of the river otters recently reintroduced to the area.

Horseback riding is allowed. To use the path beside the new trail surface between Ansonia and Tiadaghton, equestrians should park at the Ansonia Trail head.

Near Ansonia, park at Darlington Run on Route 362 just before its intersection with Route 6; or turn left at the intersection of Routes 6 and 362, cross the bridge over the Creek (and trail) and take an immediate right onto SR3022. The parking lot is on the right.

Or, park at Rattlesnake Rock on Route 414, two miles south of Blackwell to ride north on the trail. A small parking lot is avalable at Blackwell. The trail is not yet open north of Ansonia or south of Rattlesnake Rock.

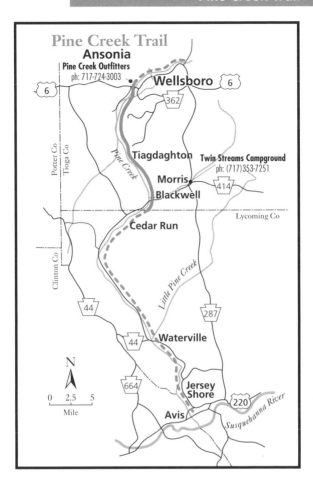

Pine Creek Trail

Ansonia
Pine Creek Outfitters
ph: 717-724-3003

Wellsboro

Potter Co
Tioga Co

Pine Creek

Tiagdaghton

Twin Streams Campground
ph: (717)353-7251

Morris
Blackwell

Lycoming Co

Cedar Run

Clinton Co

Little Pine Creek

Waterville

N

0   2.5   5
Mile

Jersey Shore

Avis

Susquehanna River

Location:	Tioga and Lycoming Counties
Miles:	20
Endpoints:	Ansonia to Blackwell
Surface:	Crushed limestone
Contact:	Bureau of Forestry
	Tioga State Forest
	Wellsboro, PA 16901
	717-724-2868

Plainfield Township Trail

Once used to transport slate from nearby quarries, the Bangor and Portland Railway opened in 1880 and ran from the Delaware, Lackawanna and Western's main line at Portland.

A formal merger of the Bangor and Portland and the Delaware, Lackawanna and Western Railroad occurred on July 1, 1909. One of the last branches to operate steam locomotives, the Bangor Engine Terminal withdrew its last steam locomotive on January 5, 1953.

The railroad was bought by Conrail in 1976, and then abandoned in 1981. It was sold to Plainfield Township in 1987 and converted to a trail.

A breathtaking view of a 70-foot drop into the Bushkill Creek is just one of the features this trail has to offer. Traversing the entire length of the township, the 60-foot wide right-of-way may eventually link at least seven other trails, including the Appalachian Trail, to create a corridor from the Lehigh and Delaware Valleys to the Poconos.

For now, there are miles of rural landscapes and beautiful views to behold as you wind your way through the countryside and over the Bushkill's five bridges.

To reach the Belfast Junction parking lot, take the Stockertown Exit off of Route 33 and make a right at the first stop sign. At the next traffic light, turn left onto Sullivan Trail Road. Travel .75 of a mile past a power station on the right. The Belfast Junction trail head parking lot will be on your right.

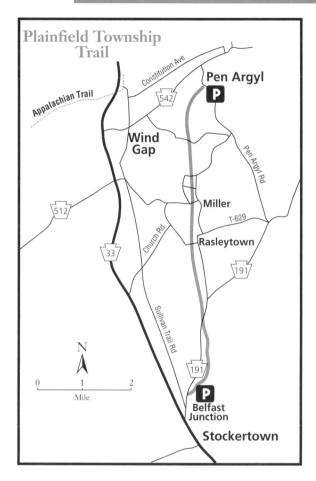

Plainfield Township
Trail

Appalachian Trail

Constitution Ave

Pen Argyl
P

542

**Wind
Gap**

Pen Argyl Rd

512

Miller

T-629

33

Church Rd

Rasleytown

191

Sullivan Trail Rd

N

0   1   2
Mile

191

P

**Belfast
Junction**

Stockertown

Location: Northampton County
Miles: 6.7
Endpoints: Plainfield Township to Pen Argyl
Surface: Crushed stone
Contact: Ginny Koehler
 Plainfield Township
 6292 Sullivan Trail
 Nazareth, PA 18064
 610-759-6944

PW&S Railroad Hiking-Biking Trail

The Pittsburgh, Westmoreland & Somerset Railroad (PW&S) was chartered in 1899 to transport oak, hickory, cherry, and hemlock to a sawmill in Ligonier.

In 1901, a passenger coach and flatcars were added to the railroad so that people could travel along to picnic on the mountain. Although the passengers were sprayed with cinders and jolted on hard wooden floors, they paid 50 cents for a round trip ticket.

The railroad was abandoned in 1916 and reopened as a hiking trail in 1992.

Located in Forbes State Forest and Linn Run State Park, on the PW&S Railroad Hiking-Biking Trail you will step back in time as you discover how the creek gurgling next to you and the tall oak and cherry trees towering above you were vital to the railroaders and their families 70 years before.

Each historical landmark and the natural resources associated with it are noted and explained on a posted sign. Some of the landmarks on the trail include stone-work remains of the old sawmill, the mill race and the stone abutment for a bridge over Linn Run.

Linn Run Road is located east of Ligonier on US30. Go 2 miles and, at PA381, turn right. Go 3 miles to Linn Run Road in Rector, turn left onto Linn Run Rd, travel 4 miles to the start of Quarry Trail, and park in parking lot. You can follow Linn Run Rd to the top of the mountain, Beam Run Trail.

For the Laurel Mountain trailhead, go east on US30 8 miles from Ligonier. As 30 crests the ridge, turn right at the AT&T towers onto Laurel Summit Rd. Another .4 miles farther is an additional parking lot. Please note that this trail is used as a road.

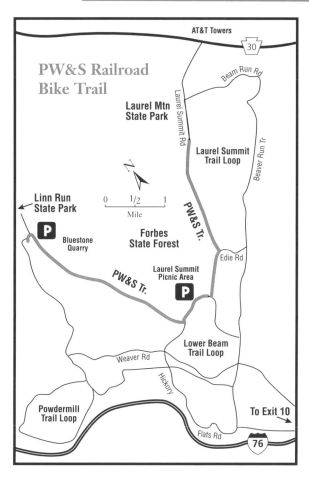

PW&S Railroad
Bike Trail

Laurel Mtn
State Park

Laurel Summit
Trail Loop

Linn Run
State Park

P

Bluestone
Quarry

Forbes
State Forest

PW&S Tr.

PW&S Tr.

Laurel Summit
Picnic Area

P

Edie Rd

Lower Beam
Trail Loop

Weaver Rd

Hickory

Powdermill
Trail Loop

Flats Rd

To Exit 10

Laurel Summit Rd

Beam Run Rd

Beaver Run Tr

AT&T Towers

30

76

N

0   1/2   1
Mile

  on the 2.5-mile section

    on the 29-mile section

 on certain sections of
the 29-mile section

Location: Westmoreland and Somerset Counties
Miles: 9.5
Endpoints: Linn Run State Park
to Laurel Mountain State Park
Surface: Dirt Road
Contact: Loyalhanna Watershed Association
PO Box 561
Ligonier, PA 15658
724-238-7560

Pymatuning State Park Trail

The word "Pymatuning"" is derived from the Iroquois language, probably from the Seneca tribe, meaning "the crooked-mouthed man's dwelling place." This saying may refer to the Erie tribe, which previously lived in the area and was ruled by a queen known for her cunning.

The trail is located on the abandoned Erie and Pittsburgh branch of the Pennsylvania Railroad and is partially located in Pymatuning State Park. The park was created in 1931 as plans to dam Pymatuning Lake were finalized. Today, it is a very popular two-state recreational area.

Although the trail is short, 2.3 miles in length, points of interest located adjacent to it make it a worthwhile experience. The trail is notable for passing the Pymatuning Lake spillway where you can feed the fish and geese that cluster there. You'll also find a waterfowl museum and fish hatchery with visitors centers at both locations. At the visitors centers, you can learn about the many species that are protected in the 2,500 acre wildlife refuge adjacent to the lake. These facilities are generally open from late spring through early fall.

The trailhead is located one mile south of Linesville off the Linesville/Hartstown Road located between SR 6 and SR 285.

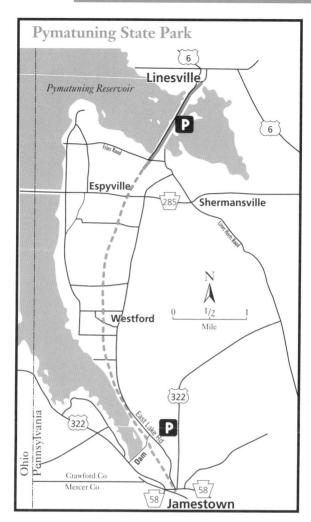

Pymatuning State Park

Location:	Crawford County
Miles:	2.3
Endpoints:	Pymatuning State Park
Surface:	Cinder, grass
Contact:	Pymatuning State Park
	PO Box 425
	Jamestown, PA 16134
	724-932-3141
	www.dcnr.state.pa.us

Railroad Grade Trail

Originally built for the New York Central Railroad, this grade was relocated when the Tioga-Hammond Lakes were created by building the Tioga Dam and the Hammond Dam, two of 14 dams operated by the US Army Corps of Engineers (Baltimore District). The original railroad bed then became part of the Ives Run Recreation Area and opened in 1979.

A birdwatcher's delight, this leisurely trail is best explored with binoculars. With Crooked Creek on your right and state game lands on your left, you'll observe a variety of songbirds, waterfowl, and gamebirds as you travel through the Bryant Hollow Wildlife Management Area.

Other trails in the area include a one-mile loop archery trail, which offers twelve stations and two tree stands to practice your archery skills, the Stephenhouse Trail with markers identifying numerous trees, and the Lynn Keller Hiking Trail for the serious hiker who enjoys steep climbs.

Enter Ives Run Recreation Area off PA287 between Tioga and Holiday. Turn right at road to administration building (archery range) then immediately right onto gravel road and the beginning of the trail. The trail is closed April to August for osprey breeding.

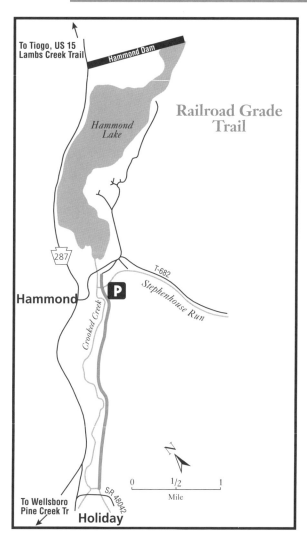

(trail is also open to automobiles from mid-April to Memorial Day and October through December)

Location:	Tioga County
Miles:	2.6
Endpoints:	Ives Run Recreation Area to Holiday
Surface:	Stone and gravel
Contact:	US Army Corps of Engineers
	RR 1, Box 65
	Tioga, PA 16946-9733
	717-835-5281

Roaring Run Trail

The Roaring Run Trail was built on the abandoned Pennsylvania Railroad Apollo Industrial Track which was built on the abandoned Pennsylvania West Branch Canal. Today, portions of the canal can still be seen from the trail.

The Roaring Run Watershed Association was formed in 1982 to help preserve this historic area and clean up pollution from abandoned mines. The right of way was donated to the association and opened as a trail in 1989.

Beginning at the parking area on Canal Road, the Roaring Run Trail parallels the Kiskiminetas River to the southeast. At the 1.5-mile mark, the remains of canal guard lock No. 15 can be seen. Directly out from these remains once stood a 16-foot high dam. the dam was destroyed in a flood in 1866; however, during low water some remains area visible.

Take US66 north to Apollo. After crossing the Kiskiminetas River, turn right at the first traffic light onto Kiskiminetas Avenue. Go through town to Cherry Lane and take the right fork onto Canal Road instead of going up the hill. The road ends at the trailhead parking lot, 1.3 miles from the traffic light in Apollo.

DID YOU KNOW?

❏ There are nearly 800 miles of rail-trail in the state of Pennsylvania alone!

❏ As of September 1998, there were 987 rail-trails in the United States—more than 10,076 miles of rail-trail!

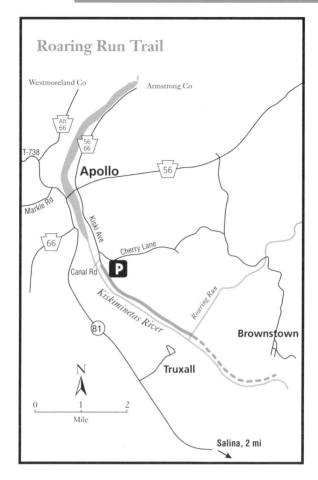

Roaring Run Trail

Westmoreland Co

Armstrong Co

Alt 66

56 66

T-738

56

Apollo

Markle Rd

Kiski Ave

Cherry Lane

66

Canal Rd

P

Roaring Run

Kiskiminetas River

81

Brownstown

N

Truxall

0   1   2
Mile

Salina, 2 mi

Location:	Armstrong County
Miles:	3.7 (2.0 complete)
Endpoints:	Canal Road to Roaring Run
Surface:	Crushed limestone
Contact:	Andy Schreffler
	Roaring Run Watershed Association
	215 Rovel Street
	Apollo, PA 15686
	724-568-1483

Samuel Justus Recreational Trail

Connecting Oil City and Franklin, the Samuel Justus Recreational Trail is a 6-mile segment of a 30-mile trail that follows what was originally the Allegheny Valley Railroad.

The "A.V." was completed to Oil City in 1868 and connected the oil fields with Pittsburgh. It operated as an independent company until it was absorbed into the Pennsylvania Railroad system in 1910. The line was abandoned by Conrail in 1984.

The trail begins across the Allegheny River from Franklin, known for its well-preserved Victorian architecture and tree-lined streets. The trail follows the river north toward Oil City through lush woodlands, passing iron furnaces, several operating oil wells, Pioneer Cemetery, an orchard planted by Johnny Appleseed, and a visitor's center located in an 1844 Salt Box house.

The trail's paved surface is perfect for bicycling and in-line skating. You may also want to visit the mansion of Senator Joseph Sibley, who made his fortune by inventing the first formula for refining crude oil.

To access the trail in Franklin, take PA8 north to its juncture with US322. Take US322 as it becomes 8th Street and crosses the Allegheny River. Trailhead parking is on the right after the bridge. The parking lot is marked for the Samuel Justus Trail and is also the only trailhead for the Allegheny River Trail (see page 12). For Oil City access, stay on US62/PA8 about 8 miles to Oil City. Follow 62 north as it turns right and crosses the river, then turn right at the second light onto West First Street. Go about 1.6 miles to just past the Penelec plant. Turn right and follow the road to the parking lot.

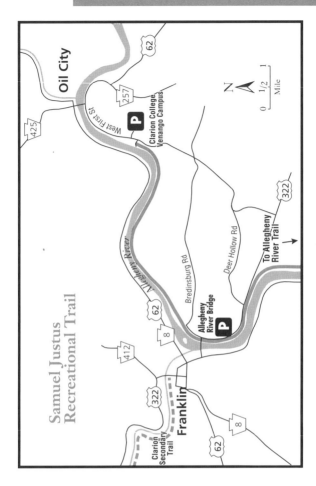

Location: Venango County
Miles: 5.8
Endpoints: Franklin to Oil City
Surface: Asphalt
Contact: Cranberry Township
PO Box 378
Seneca, PA 16346
814-676-8812

Schuylkill River Trail

The Schuylkill River Trail is a rails-to-trails project that began in the 1970s. The trail runs along an old Pennsylvania Railroad line, even though Conrail still uses parallel sections of the right-of-way.

The trail stretches 25 miles along the historic Schuylkill River from Independence Hall in Philadelphia to Valley Forge National Historical Park. At Valley Forge you can continue traveling north by linking with the Betzwood Trail. This trail will eventually join with others in Berks and Schuylkill Counties to create more than 100 continuous miles of rail-trail along the Schuylkill River, from Philadelphia to the coal regions near Pottsville.

The trail traverses beautiful scenic and natural areas of the lower Schuylkill River. Heading southeast from the Betzwood Trail, you'll pass Sythane Taylor, the site of a 1930s film studio where westerns were produced.

Riverfront Park in Norristown is a good place to rest and enjoy the view of the river. Continuing on the trail you'll notice deep cuts exposing limestone and dolomite rock formations. Arriving in Spring Mill, you might want to spend some time at the Schuylkill Center for Environmental Education. In Manayunk, follow the historic canal, which was part of the Schuylkill Navigation System from Philadelphia to Port Carbon. To get to Center City Philadelphia, use the trail paralleling Kelly Drive.

To reach Valley Forge National Historical Park, take the Pennsylvania Turnpike to Exit 24 (Valley Forge). Take US422 west to Audubon Trooper Exit and turn left off the exit ramp. Parking for the Schuylkill River Trail at Betzwood is just ahead on the right.

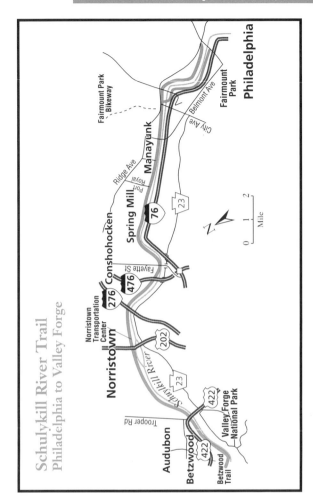

Schulykill River Trail
Philadelphia to Valley Forge

Location:	Philadelphia and Montgomery Counties
Miles:	25
Endpoints:	Philadelphia to Valley Forge
Surface:	Asphalt
Contact:	John H. Wood
	Montgomery County Planning Commission
	Montgomery County Courthouse
	PO Box 311
	Norristown, PA 19404-0311
	610-278-3736

Sentiero di Shay

Located in the northwest corner of Lycoming County near the village of Slate Run, the Black Forest was named for the dense, dark coniferous forests that originally covered the region. Now a part of the Tiadaghton State Forest, the Black Forest Trail system is a 42-mile series of loop trails comprised partially of the remains of the Cammal and Black Forest Railroad, the Slate Run Railroad and logging roads.

The Sentiero di Shay Trail (whose name translates from Italian as "path of Shay") pays tribute to the Italian laborers who hand-built the railroad grade so that timber might be transported by rugged Shay engines.

Primarily a cross-country ski route, this 13-mile trail can also be enjoyed for hiking. You'll pass oak, white birch, pitch pine, several aspen meadows, streams and hollows, a spruce corridor, and other diverse hardwoods. Along the way, the Sentiero di Shay shares the railroad corridor with another cross-country ski trail, the George B. Will Trail. Mr. Will was a ranger for the Forest Service who is credited with introducing cross-country skiing to the area in 1914 on skis imported from Sweden. Much of the Black Forest had been cut over by that time and George recalled that "you could see for miles."

Joining the Black Forest Trail System and the Susquehannock Trail System, are the North and South Link Trails, 9.3 and 6 miles respectively. Built almost exclusively on abandoned railroad grades, the Link Trails help provide a roughly 26-mile (two or three day) backpacking loop traversing three counties, numerous water courses, and countless cross trails and abandoned railroad grades.

To reach the trailhead, take PA44 slightly more than one-half mile south of Slate Run Road, 34 miles south of Coudersport. The trail begins at the trailhead for the Blackberry Trail, designated by a carved wooden sign. The Sentiero di Shay is blazed with blue circles.

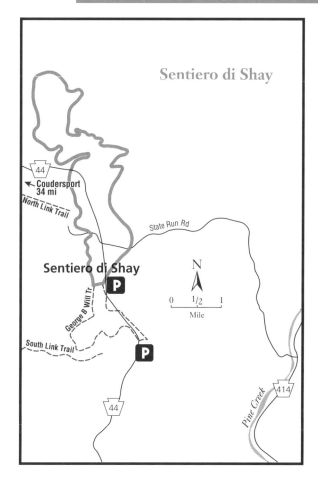

Location: Lycoming County
Miles: 13.4
Endpoints: Within Tiadaghton State Forest
Surface: Grass
Contact: Tiadaghton State Forest
Bureau of Forestry
423 East Central Avenue
South Williamsport, PA 17701
717-327-3450

Stavich Bicycle Trail

The Stavich Trail is unusual for two reasons. First, unlike most rail-trails, it was built on an abandoned interurban electric railroad right of way: the Penn-Ohio line which was abandoned in 1933. Interurbans were not built to the stringent standards of conventional railroads, so you'll encounter more grades than you might on an ordinary rail-trail.

The Stavich's second notable feature is the fact that it is one of the few rail-trails in the country that connects two states. This gently rolling trail will take you from Struthers, Ohio to near New Castle, Pennsylvania.

Running along the Mahoning River, this mostly rural trail also parallels the CSX railroad main line. The asphalt-paved trail is great for bicycling, in-line skating, walking and is accessible for persons with disabilities.

This 12-mile trail was constructed in 1983 with the help of donations from the Stavich family and local individuals.

On the Pennsylvania side, take PA60 north to US224 west (Sampson Street) and follow US224 toward Poland. After .7 miles, turn left on Covert Road (SR3010) at the ballfield. Follow Covert Road 1.4 miles to the trailhead. For Ohio, stay on US224 10.5 miles to Poland. Turn right on OH616 across the Mahoning River and immediately turn right on OH289. Stay on 289 (Broad Street) 1.1 miles to trailhead parking.

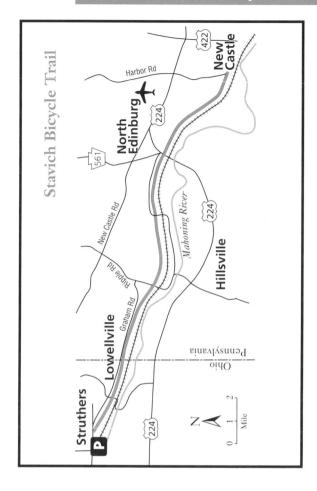

Location:	Lawrence (PA) and Mahoning (OH) Counties
Miles:	12
Endpoints:	New Castle, PA to Struthers, OH
Surface:	Asphalt
Contact:	JoAnne McBride
	Lawrence County Tourism Bureau
	229 South Jefferson Street
	New Castle, PA 16101
	724-654-8408

Stony Valley Railroad Grade

Named St. Anthony's Wilderness by Moravian missionaries who came in 1742 to convert native tribes, the Stony Creek valley became the site of five bustling towns after discovery of coal in 1824. The 1850s saw the construction of the Schuylkill & Susquehanna Railroad, built to transport coal to the canals and tourists to Cold Springs' famous mineral water. So popular was the spring water that a 200-room resort was built to accommodate the wealthy Philadelphians who came for the healing waters.

By 1944, the mines were exhausted, the lumber stripped, the railroad abandoned, and the hotel burned as the last residents left. The Pennsylvania Game Commission purchased the land in 1945 and converted the railroad to a trail soon after, making the Stony Valley Railroad Grade one of the nation's first rail-trails.

Located in 44,342 acres of state game land, the forest has rebounded in a remarkable way, providing habitat for an abundance of animals and preserving what remains of the mining towns. The foundation and stone steps to the old Cold Springs Hotel stand shaded by towering Norway spruces originally planted by hotel landscapers.

You may hear the gurgling of an underground stream flowing over rocks in the Rattling Run area or the moans of the ghost of the headless railroad worker, known to stalk the railroad bed at night. If ghosts aren't spooky enough, search for the Rausch Gap Cemetery and its four grave markers dating back to 1854. Peaceful, yet brimming with sight and sound, Stony Creek is an experience not to be missed.

Take 22/322 north from Harrisburg, exiting at Route 225 into Dauphin. Just after the exit, the road veers left and crosses Stony Creek. Turn right onto Stony Creek Road and follow it for 5 miles to what appears to be a cul-de-sac. At the top of the cul-de-sac's loop is a dirt road off to the right. Stay on this dirt road to the trailhead.

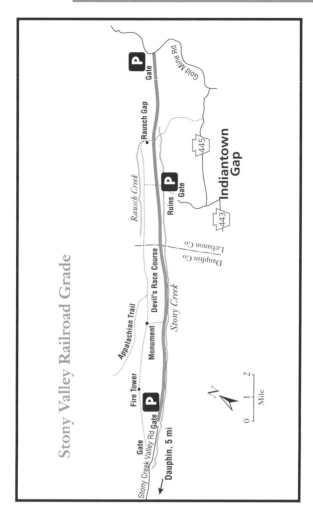

Stony Valley Railroad Grade

Location:	Dauphin, Lebanon and Schuylkill Counties
Miles:	18
Endpoints:	Dauphin to Gold Mine Rd.
Surface:	Packed cinder/dirt
Contact:	Roland Bergner, Chief Federal/State Coordination Division Pennsylvania Game Commission 2001 Elmerton Avenue Harrisburg, PA 17110-9797 717-787-9612

Struble Trail

Originally a branch of the Pennsylvania Railroad, the abandoned right-of-way was converted into a trail by the Chester County Parks & Recreation Department in 1979. Today the 2.5-mile trail attracts 50,000 visitors each year. The county hopes to extend the trail to include 15.5 more miles.

Paralleling the east branch of Brandywine Creek, the Struble Trail provides a perfect setting for amateur naturalists and wonderful opportunities for anglers, joggers, and bicyclists. Equestrians are welcome on the undeveloped sections of the trail.

While you're in the area, you may want to visit the other parks located in Chester County. Hibernia County Park offers 800 acres of woodlands and meadows for picnicking and camping. There are plenty of good fishing spots along the west branch of Brandywine Creek and children's pond stocked with trout from the park's nursery. There are also seasonal tours of Hibernia Mansion and Hatfield House, an ironmaster's county home listed on the National Register of Historic Places.

Springton Manor Farm, which was part of William Penn Manor, is also included in the National Register of Historic Places and is a tourist demonstration farm that includes animal petting areas and an agricultural museum.

From US Route 30 bypass traveling west, exit at Route 282 near Downingtown. Turn left off the exit, proceed under the Route 30 bridge. The trailhead is the second drive on the right. From US Route 30 Bypass traveling east, exit at US322, turn right and go to Pennsylvania Avenue in Downingtown. Turn left and proceed to another left on PA282. Turn right onto Norwood Road; the trailhead is the first left.

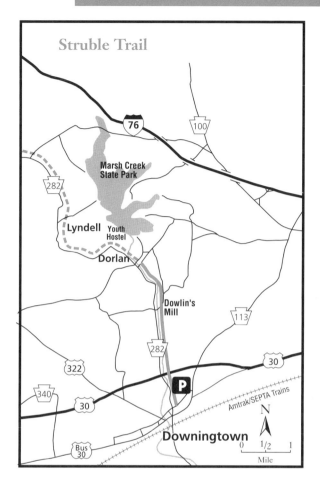

 on certain sections

Location:	Chester County
Miles:	2.5
Endpoints:	Downingtown to Honeybrook
Surface:	Asphalt
Contact:	Chester County Parks & Recreation
	601 Westtown Road
	West Chester, PA 16382
	610-344-6415

Susquehannock Trail System

Located in scenic Potter and Clinton Counties, the Susquehannock Hiking Trail is an 85 mile amalgamation of old Civilian Conservation Corps fire trails, logging roads and railroad grades through the Susquehannock State Forest. Isolated and pristine, the Susquehannock Trail System provides hikers and backpackers a well-marked (orange blazed) trail with few steep grades and even fewer signs of "civilization." The Hammersley Wild Area is especially unspoiled, offering the longest section of roadless trail in the Susquehannock loop.

Somewhat coincidentally, the Hammersley is also the most rail-intensive portion of the system. Timber was cut here between 1906 and 1910. Several logging camps and a small town were once located near where Nelson Branch and Hammersley Fork merge. Also, this site is just north of the Forrest H. Dutlinger Natural Area, a 1,500 acre preserve which includes a 158-acre stand of old growth timber (primarily hemlocks).

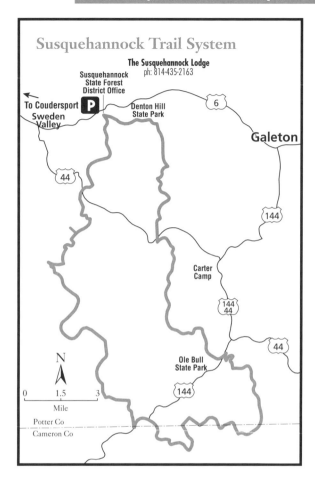

Location: Potter and Clinton Counties
Miles: Roughly 30 miles of rail-trail
Endpoints: Loop trail in Susquehannock State Forest
Surface: Grass and dirt
Contact: Susquehannock State Forest
Bureau of Forestry
3150 East 2nd St.
PO Box 673
Coudersport, PA 16915-0673
814-274-8474

119

Switchback Railroad Trail

The Switchback Railroad was the second railroad operating in America and the first in Pennsylvania when it opened in May 1927. Built to haul coal from the Summit Mine to the Lehigh Canal, the railroad had evolved by 1944 from a gravity and mule-powered system to a 95% gravity-run operation (with the help of two steam engines).

Although the cars ceased carrying coal in 1932, they continued to haul people, who came to enjoy the thrilling ride. Thomas Edison was one of those people, as was the builder of the first rollercoaster. A popular tourist attraction for 59 years, the Switchback was sold for scrap in 1937 and converted to a trail in 1977.

Traversing the valley between Pisgah Mountain to the north and Mauch Chunk Ridge to the south, the trail loops down into Jim Thorpe and back up the valley to Summit Hill. Oak, hickory, and birch are found in the lower section of the valley; white pine and hemlock are nestled between the high mountain ridges. In these areas, you may observe black bear, wild turkey, porcupine, weasel, and maybe even a wildcat. Fields and streams along the trail support deer, ruffed grouse, woodchuck, red and gray foxes, beaver, and pheasant.

To access the Switchback, take US209 to Jim Thorpe. It's convenient, if not easy, to park at the railroad station downtown. Travel a few blocks west on Broadway, then turn right at the Opera House on the appropriately named Hill Road. In less than half a mile uphill, you will turn left onto the trail.

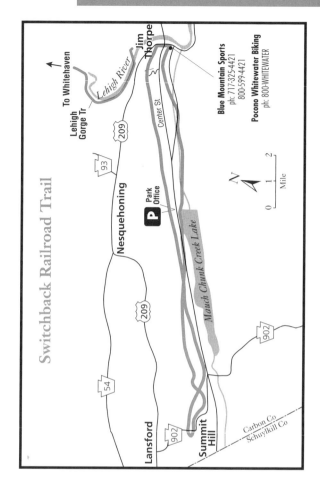

Switchback Railroad Trail

Jim Thorpe

To Whitehaven

Lehigh River

Lehigh Gorge Tr

Blue Mountain Sports
ph: 717-325-4421
800-594-4421

Pocono Whitewater Biking
ph: 800-WHITEWATER

Center St

209

93

Nesquehoning

Park Office

P

Mauch Chunk Creek Lake

209

N

0   1   2
Mile

54

Lansford

902

Summit Hill

Carbon Co
Schuylkill Co

902

Location:	Carbon County
Miles:	15
Endpoints:	Summit Hill to Jim Thorpe
Surface:	Original ballast
Contact:	Mauch Chunk Lake Park Office
	Carbon County Parks & Recreation
	625 Lentz Trail Road
	Jim Thorpe, PA 18229-1902
	717-325-3669
	www.dcnr.state.pa.us

Three Rivers Heritage Trail

The Three Rivers Heritage Trail begins in Washington's Landing, a 42-acre island in the Allegheny River. Once known as Herr's Island and a stopover for livestock trains between Chicago and the East Coast, Herr's Island has been undergoing renovation since the 1980s. Its slaughterhouses and scrap yards have been replaced by office buildings, a marina, tennis courts, and a trail circling the island. Traveling down the Allegheny to the Ohio River, past Roberto Clemente Park and the Carnegie Science Center, then crossing the Ohio and proceeding up the Monongahela past Station Square and Southside Riverfront Park, it's easy to see how the Three Rivers Heritage Trail will link the most dynamic geographic and historical features of this vibrant city. Offering precisely the kind of transportation alternatives to which Rails-to-Trails Conservancy and its supporting organizations are most committed, the Three Rivers Heritage Trail will also provide a vital link to the Pittsburgh to Washington, DC trail sought for completion by 1999.

There are presently three sections of trail completed, totaling 4.4 miles. The largest section of 2.5 miles runs from the Carnegie Science Center to Washington's Landing. Park at Three Rivers Stadium or the Science Center. Once you reach the river's edge at Washington's Landing, a soon-to-be opened pedestrian/bicycling bridge takes you to the island, where another mile of trail encircles it. Parking is available on Washington's Landing. For the .8-mile Southside Riverfront Park segment, take East Carson Street to 18th and turn toward the river. Cross the tracks and go upstream to parking just after the boat ramp under the Birmingham Bridge.

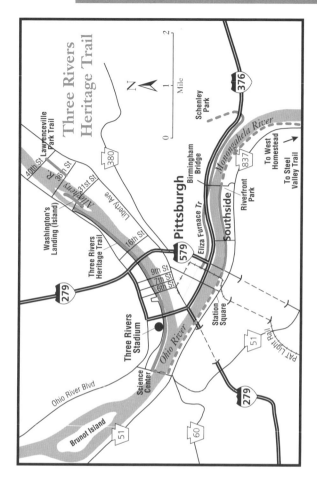

Location: Allegheny County
Miles: 4.4 miles
Endpoints: Washington's Landing to
Carnegie Science Center
Surface: Crushed limestone and asphalt
Contact: John Stephen
Friends of the Riverfront
PO Box 42434
Pittsburgh, PA 15203
412-488-0212
www.atatrail.org

Thun Trail

Declared Pennsylvania's first Scenic River by the state legislature in 1978, the Schuylkill River flows 128 miles from the hard coal regions of Schuylkill County to the Delaware River in Philadelphia. The Thun (pronounced "Tune") Trail is the first step in an ambitious and historic effort to link the river's five counties in a greenway of parks and trails.

The trail follows the former Pennsylvania Railroad Schuylkill Branch and parallels the route of the historic Schuylkill Canal. Today one can see many reminders of the corridor's watery heritage. Restoration of a century-old stone culvert over Dick's Run and of two concrete multiple arch bridges over the Schuylkill Rover (built in 1918) have been completed. On these and other projects, dedicated volunteers aided professionals in the development of the trail. Near the trail in Gibraltar, the Allegheny Aqueduct was built in 1824 to carry the Schuylkill Canal across the Allegheny Creek. A link to this site is planned.

Paralleling highly congested Routes 422 and 724, the Thun Trail offers a welcome respite for commuters seeking an alternate path to work and leisure activities. Currently 2.5 miles of trail are open with work on the remaining sections to begin in the near future.

To reach the trailhead near Reading, take Route 10 (Morgantown Road) .9 mile east from the intersection of Routes 222 (Lancaster Avenue) and 10. Parking is on the north side of Route 10, opposite Orrton Avenue.

In Gibraltar, parking is available near the PennDOT Park and Ride at the intersection of Routes 176 and 724. The trail is located where the railroad crossed Route 724 at Ridgewood. A kiosk and PennDOT salt sheds are visible from the road.

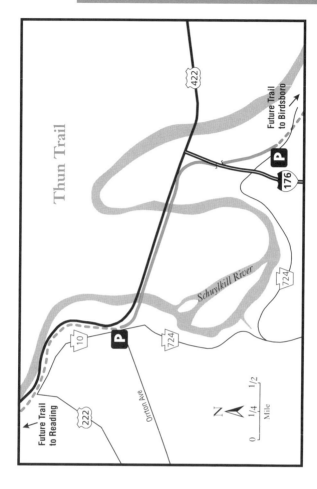

Location:	Berks County
Miles:	10.0
Endpoints:	West Reading to Stowe
Surface:	Crushed stone and original ballast on 2.5 mile open trail
Contact:	Jim Bosjolie Schuylkill River Greenway Association 960 Old Mill Road Wyomissing, PA 19610 610-372-3916

Towpath Bike Trail

Three modes of transportation once operated on the Towpath Bike Trail: the Lehigh Canal, the Central Railroad of New Jersey (Easton and Western branch), and the Lehigh Valley Transit interurban.

Chartered in 1818, the privately-owned canal remained in operation for 113 years. It hauled anthracite coal from Mauch Chunk to the Delaware Canal at Easton. The Easton and Western branch was built in 1914 and abandoned in 1972. The LVT Easton line was part of a larger electric railway system that stretched from the Delaware Water Gap to near Philadelphia.

This trail (formerly known as the "National Trails Towpath Bike Trail of Palmer and Bethlehem Townships") offers a smorgasbord of activities and scenery.

The trail hosts 70,000 people annually, the majority coming from Palmer and Bethlehem Townships, as well as residents of Northampton and Lehigh Counties. Nearly 30% of the trail users are people commuting to and from work, school, shopping areas, and parks.

This eight-foot wide asphalt trail starts near the Easton Area High School and traverses a variety of landscapes, including forests, farmland, residential neighborhoods, and the banks of the Lehigh River.

The trail also provided some land along the river, which is now Riverview Park, a popular fishing area that provides access to the Delaware and Lehigh Canal National Heritage Corridor.

For parking at Riverview Park, take US Route 22 east from SR33 to 25th Street South. Stay on 25th Street South for about two miles and turn right on Lehigh Street. Turn right into the parking lot.

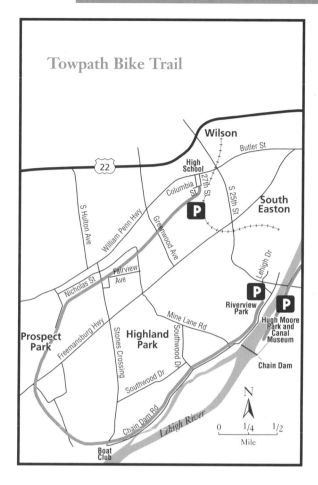

Location: Northampton County
Miles: 7.8
Endpoints: Bethlehem to Palmer
Surface: Asphalt
Contact: Ted Borek
           Palmer Township Board of Supervisors
           PO Box 3039
           Palmer, PA 18043
           215-253-7191

Warren-North Warren Bike Trail

Located along the banks of the Conewango Creek, the open two mile segment of this proposed 2 mile trail follows an old New York Central branch from the City of Warren north. Designed to serve first as a safe alternative for cyclists and commuters from the downtown area to a burgeoning business district along Route 62, the Warren-North Warren Bike Trail will also serve to preserve the scenic vistas of the Conewango and control flooding along its tributary, Jackson Run.

The railroad that will become the Warren/North Warren Trail was built to provide rail service to the several oil refineries which once occupied this area. The existing trail follows the banks of the beautiful Conewango Creek.

Take Business Route 6 (Pennsylvania Avenue in Warren) to its intersection with Market Street (Route 62N). Go to Fifth Avenue, proceed east one block to East Street. Turn left and go to the trailhead at the end of East Street. To reach the other trailhead, continue north on Route 62 to Jackson Street in North Warren.

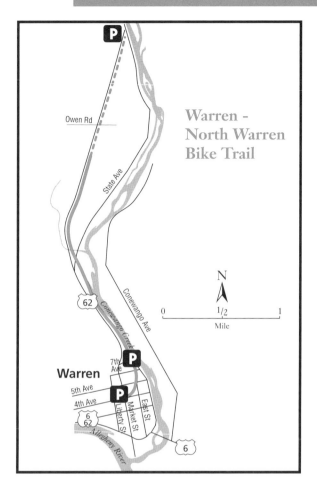

Warren -
North Warren
Bike Trail

Owen Rd

State Ave

62

Conewango Ave

Conewango Creek

N

0   1/2   1
Mile

Warren

7th Ave

5th Ave

4th Ave

East St

Market St

Liberty St

6
62

Allegheny River

6

Location:	Warren County	
Miles:	2	
Endpoints:	Warren to North Warren	
Surface:	Asphalt	
Contact:	Dan Glotz	
	Warren County Planning &	
	Zoning Commission	
	207 W. 5th Ave	
	Warren, PA 16365	
	814-726-3861	

129

York County Heritage Rail-Trail

The York Heritage Rail-Trail's ten miles link with Maryland's Northern Central Rail-Trail to provide a 30-mile journey through southcentral Pennsylvania and northcentral Maryland's farmlands and forests. And they aren't finished yet! The York Heritage Rail-Trail Authority has its sights set on the City of York and its colonial-era courthouse downtown.

The 19th century saw the growth of the Northern Central Railroad, a vital link between Washington, DC, Harrisburg, upstate New York and Lake Ontario. Its passage through York County brought prosperity to the area's farmers, merchants and manufacturers and spurred the growth of communities like Glen Rock, Hanover Junction and the aptly-named town of Railroad along winding Codorus Creek.

The railroad was also a prime target for the Confederate Army prior to the Battle of Gettysburg, as Rebel troops cut telegraph wires and destroyed bridges in their efforts to isolate Washington from the rest of the Union. After the tragic Battle, President Lincoln traveled via the Northern Central to the battlefield, his train stopping in Hanover Junction where Matthew Brady took a photograph showing, according to many, the President standing outside the station.

After the war, the railroad remained a vital link between the nation's prosperous cities. Passengers could leave York and make their way to Baltimore and Washington to the south, Chicago and St. Louis to the west, and Buffalo and New York to the north. Since this is a rails-with-trails project, trail users can ride or walk the trail by day and ride along it on weekend evenings on a dinner train.

Hanover Junction is located on SR616 north of Glen Rock. From Interstate 83, take Exit 3 (Loganville). Follow signs to 214. Continue west on 214 for approximately 5 miles to 616 South. Follow 616 South. Rail-trail parking lot is approximately one mile on the left. For an alternate route from York, take Route 30 West to 616 South. Hanover Junction is 6.5 miles on the left.

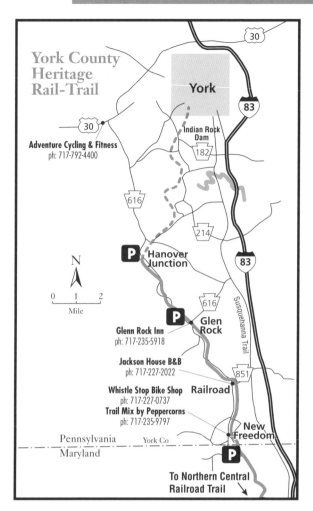

York County
Heritage
Rail-Trail

York

Indian Rock
Dam

Adventure Cycling & Fitness
ph: 717-792-4400

N

0 1 2
Mile

Hanover
Junction

Glenn Rock Inn
ph: 717-235-5918

Glen
Rock

Jackson House B&B
ph: 717-227-2022

Whistle Stop Bike Shop
ph: 717-227-0737

Railroad

Trail Mix by Peppercorns
ph: 717-235-9797

New
Freedom

Pennsylvania   York Co
Maryland

To Northern Central
Railroad Trail

Susquehanna Trail

Location:	York County
Miles:	10.7
Endpoints:	Hanover Junction to Maryland border
Surface:	Crushed limestone
Contact:	Gwen Loose
	York County Rail-Trail Authority
	5922 Nixon Dr
	York, PA 17403
	717-428-2586

Youghiogheny River Trail (North)

Built in 1883, the Pittsburgh, McKeesport and Youghiogheny hauled coal and coke from the rich Connellsville District to the steel mills of Pittsburgh. Nicknamed the "P-Mickey" for its initials, P. McK. & Y., it was merged into the Pittsburgh and Lake Erie Railroad in 1965 and became known as the Connellsville Branch.

The freight and coal traffic that sustained the branch dried up by the mid-1980s and the line was abandoned in 1990. It was immediately purchased by the Regional Trail Corporation, a three-county consortium that is building and operating the trail.

The development of this north section of the Youghiogheny River Trail (YRT) will help complete a multi-state rail-trail system linking Pittsburgh to Washington, DC. The 13.5 mile section between Smithton and Dawson should be completed by late fall, 1998, and the entire 43 mile YRT, North should be completed by 1999. The trail is especially suited to long-distance leisure trips, since the rise in elevation is no more than 100 feet for the entire trail.

Parking is available in several places along the trail. For the northern trailhead at Boston, take PA51 southeast from Pittsburgh to PA48. Turn north on 48 at Round Hill Regional Park and travel about 8 miles to a five-way intersection in Boston at the Youghiogheny River. Turn left and then immediately right; the road crosses the trail in less than a block and parking is apparent. To reach the southern trailhead on this completed section in Smithton from the PA Turnpike at New Stanton, take I-70 west to the Smithton Exit; turn left to Smithton, right onto PA 981, across the Youghiogheny River, then immediately turn right into the access area. See the listing for the YRT (South) for directions to its trailhead in Connellsville, a convenient launching point for both the YRT (South) and the YRT (North) to Dawson/Dickerson Run.

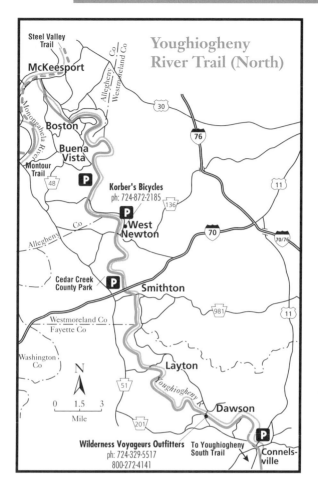

Location: Allegheny, Fayette and Westmoreland Counties

Miles: 43

Endpoints: Connellsville to McKeesport

Surface: Crushed limestone

Contact: Robert G. McKinley
Regional Trail Corporation
PO Box 95
West Newton, PA 15089
412-872-5586
www.atatrail.com
email: yrt@nb.net

Youghiogheny River Trail (South)

This 28-mile segment of the Youghiogheny River Trail (YRT) follows the abandoned Western Maryland Railroad, which was built in 1912. It travels through Ohiopyle State Park, which was named for the Native American word "Ohiopehhle," meaning "white, frothy water."

In 1754, George Washington came down the Yough (pronounced "Yock") hoping to capture Fort Duquesne, but he abandoned all efforts when he saw the great falls at Ohiopyle. Today, Ohiopyle State Park encompasses approximately 19,052 acres of beautiful river scenery and serves as the gateway to the Laurel Mountains. The Youghiogheny River Gorge, famous for its whitewater rafting and kayaking, winds through the park and the YRT (South) follows the river through Ohiopyle State Park from near Connellsville to Confluence.

The Ohiopyle trailhead is located at a restored railroad station serving as an information center with restrooms. Rental outlets for bicycles are located nearby.

Parking is available in Ohiopyle proper on either side of PA381. To reach the southern trailhead in Confluence, follow 381 through Ohiopyle to SR2012 and turn left. Go 8.1 miles to PA281 and turn north. When 281 crosses the Youghiogheny, either turn left onto River Road to trailhead parking at Ramcat Hollow or follow 281 across the bridge, park in Confluence itself and ride back across this bridge. For the northern trailhead in Connellsville, take US119 south into Connellsville to its intersection with PA711. Go north on 711 to Third Street, where you'll see a bike lane. Turn left on Third Street and follow the bicycle trail to parking. Third Street also forms a connector to the Youghiogheny River Trail (North).

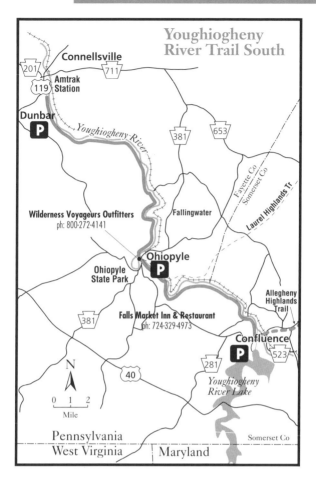

Youghiogheny
River Trail South

Location:	Fayette and Somerset Counties
Miles:	28
Endpoints:	Confluence to Connellsville
Surface:	Crushed limestone
Contact:	Ohiopyle State Park
	PO Box 105
	Ohiopyle, PA 15470
	724-329-8591
	www.atatrail.org
	www.dcnr.state.pa.us

Index to Services

The Clubhouse Bed & Breakfast   **P. 77**
327 High St.
Williamsburg, PA 16693
800-442-2990 or 814-832-9122
www.midpa-bed-breakfast.com

The Inn at Jim Thorpe   **P. 71**
24 Broadway
Jim Thorpe, PA 18229
800-329-2599
www.innjt.com

The Susquehannock Lodge   **P. 119**
5039 US 6 West
Ulysses, PA 16948
814-435-2163
www.pavisnet.com/susquelodge

The Towers Victorian Inn   **P. 29**
330 South St.
Ridgway, PA 15853
814-772-7657
www.ncentral.com/~towers

Trailside Bicycle   **P. 51**
P.O. Box 352
Vintondale, PA 15961
814-749-7990

Trail Mix by Peppercorns   **P. 131**
One West Main St.
New Freedom, PA 17349
717-235-9797
email: pepcorns@aol.com

Twin Streams Campground   **P. 95**
Rt 287 Box 236
Morris, PA 16938
717-353-7251

Valleyview Farm and Campground   **Pp. 39, 85**
RR#1 Box 1348
Waymart, PA 18472
717-448-2268

Whistle Stop Bike Shop   **P. 131**
2 E. Franklin St.
New Freedom, PA 17349
717-227-0737
email: ehbike@aol.com

Wilderness Voyageurs Outfitters   **Pp. 133, 135**
PO Box 97
Ohiopyle, PA 15470
(800) 272-4141
www.wilderness-voyageurs.com

About the Rails-to-Trails Conservancy

The mission of Rails-to-Trails Conservancy is to enhance America's communities and countrysides by converting thousands of miles of abandoned rail corridors, and connecting open space, into a nationwide network of public trails.

Established in 1985, RTC is a national nonprofit public charity with more than 7,000 members in Pennsylvania. RTC :

- notifies trail advocates and local governments of upcoming right-of-way abandonments;
- assists public and private agencies in the legalities of trail corridor acquisition;
- provides technical assistance to private citizens as well as trail planners, designers, and managers on trail design, development and protection; and
- publicizes rails-to-trails issues throughout the country.

How to Become a RTC Member

Our efforts are wholly supported by the generous contributions of its members and friends—individuals and families like you. We invite you to join today by filling out the membership form on the opposite side of this page.

Membership/Gift Membership Levels:

Individual Membership	$18
Family Membership	$25
Organization Membership	$50
Business Membership	$100
Advocate Membership	$500
Trailblazer Society Membership	$1000

As a member of RTC, you will receive the following:

- A membership in the national and state organizations
- A subscription to our newsletters
- Discounts on books, merchandise and conferences
- Additional benefits for Trailblazer Society members

Most importantly, you help support the Pennsylvania office, giving you a voice in trail development in the Commonwealth and the satisfaction that comes from helping to build a statewide network of beautiful pathways for all of us to enjoy for generations to come.

Pennsylvania's Rail-Trails

 Yes, I want to help build rail-trails in Pennsylvania. Sign me up right away so I will receive merchandise discounts and newsletters.

ORDER FORM

	PRICE	QTY.	TOTAL
Pennsylvania's Rail-Trails			
(Members: $10.95 / Non-Members: $12.95)		Subtotal	
		PA 6% Sales Tax	
	($ 1.25 per book) Shipping & Handling		
Membership			
TOTAL			

NAME _____

ADDRESS_____

CITY_____ STATE____ ZIP _____

TELEPHONE_____

GIFT MEMBERSHIP—RECIPIENT

NAME _____

ADDRESS_____

CITY_____ STATE____ ZIP _____

☐ My check to Rails-to-Trails Conservancy is enclosed.

☐ Please charge my:

☐ MasterCard

☐ VISA

Card # _____ Exp. _____

Signature _____

☐ Send me more information on the Trailblazer Society.

☐ I would like more information on how to contribute through my workplace.

140